#RULES
_OF_
ENGAGEMENT

"*#Rules_of_Engagement* is an excellent primer for Catholics new to social media and for those wanting to reboot how they behave there. A brief and substantive read, this book makes for a thorough, accessible, and informative exploration of online etiquette and Christian ethics."

Mary Pezzulo
Creator of *Steel Magnificat* and author of *Stumbling into Grace: How We Meet God in Tiny Works of Mercy*

"Ann M. Garrido helps us probe difficult and essential questions of Christian identity, core values, and social media presence. Her reflective exercises and suggested habits provide practical, concrete tools for helping us navigate this often treacherous terrain and make choices that reflect our best, most-authentic selves. It is accessible and relatable. I can't wait to use this for myself and with my students!"

Sandra Derby
Theology teacher and coordinator of Liturgy
St. Agnes Academy
Houston, Texas

#RULES
_OF_
ENGAGEMENT

8 CHRISTIAN HABITS FOR BEING GOOD AND DOING GOOD ONLINE

Ann M. Garrido

Ave Maria Press AVE Notre Dame, Indiana

Founded in 1865, Ave Maria Press is a ministry of the United States Province of Holy Cross.

www.avemariapress.com

Paperback: ISBN-13 978-1-64680-059-9

E-book: ISBN-13 978-1-64680-060-5

Cover image © Springsky / iStock / Getty Images Plus.

Cover and text design by Samantha Watson.

Printed and bound in the United States of America.

Library of Congress Cataloging-in-Publication Data
Names: Garrido, Ann, 1969- author.
Title: Rules-of-engagement : 8 Christian habits for being good and doing
   good online / Ann M. Garrido.
Description: Notre Dame, Indiana : Ave Maria Press, [2021] | Includes
   bibliographical references. | Summary: "In this book, Garrido shares
   eight practical habits, rooted in Catholic Christian teaching, that help
   readers be a force for good via social media"-- Provided by publisher.
Identifiers: LCCN 2020041629 (print) | LCCN 2020041630 (ebook) | ISBN
   9781646800599 (paperback) | ISBN 9781646800605 (ebook)
Subjects: LCSH: Communication--Religious aspects--Catholic Church. | Social
   media--Religious aspects--Catholic Church. | Online etiquette. |
   Christian ethics--Catholic authors.
Classification: LCC BX1795.C67 G37 2021 (print) | LCC BX1795.C67 (ebook)
   | DDC 395.5--dc23
LC record available at https://lccn.loc.gov/2020041629
LC ebook record available at https://lccn.loc.gov/2020041630

I would like then to invite Christians, confidently and with an informed and responsible creativity, to join the network of relationships which the digital era has made possible. This is not simply to satisfy the desire to be present, but because this network is an integral part of human life.

–Pope Benedict XVI, World Communications Day 2009

Contents

Introduction

You slide into the cacophony as easily as you slide your thumb across the screen of your phone. Standing in the checkout line. Stuck at a long red light. As you prepare to turn off the bedside lamp at night. And, without even thinking about it, you're suddenly in a sea of pings and dings, tweets and posts, "likes" and hashtags.

That last sentence would not have made sense to you fifteen years ago, and—given the pace at which technology is changing—in another fifteen minutes it might not make sense again. But at this moment in time it does, or you wouldn't have picked up this book. At this moment in time you are swimming in the world of social media.[1]

And you know something about how amazing it is. How connected it makes you feel to people you would never otherwise be able to keep in contact with. How easy it now is to get the pulse of a group or make plans with family. How many times it brings a smile to your face or a word of inspiration when you most need it in your day. At times it has felt *more* than amazing. It has felt vital. It has been a link to sanity in the midst of the

Covid-19 crisis or the fastest way to get information about loved ones after a natural disaster.

But chances are you also know something about how mean-spirited and deceitful social media can be. You need look no further than your Twitter feed, where your uncle has once again retweeted a "news" story that is anything but. Or the stream of ad hominem insults pooling in the comments section of YouTube. Or—let's be honest—the quick thumbs-up you gave the article your friend posted on Facebook. You never actually read the article and have no idea whether it is worthy or not, but she often likes your posts and you thought the headline sounded good.

Social media today makes the Wild West of the past look like a child's sandbox. It's chaotic, perplexing, and hard to tell who is calling the shots. People behave in this territory unlike the way they behave at home . . . or *is* this how they actually behave at home and we just never knew? It almost makes you want to abandon social media entirely. To retreat into a cabin in the peaceful woods, maybe to a time before the internet was ever a thing. (Did I hear someone say "television"?)

But then there is this passage in the Gospel of Matthew where Jesus challenges us to be salt and light *in the world* (Matthew 5:13-16). And a conversation Christ had with Nicodemus where he reminded Nicodemus that God's love *for the world* was so great that he came to dwell within it (John 3:16). In the Christian tradition, social media is what we might call "mission territory"—a place scarcely known to us in which much is unfamiliar and easily misunderstood, but a place where we are asked nevertheless to practice our faith. In his address for World Communications Day 2009, Pope Benedict called social media the new "digital continent" that we Christians are to enter with courage, knowing that our presence there can help shape the landscape of this still-new frontier.[2]

The vastness of the continent alone intimidates. Facebook, the largest social networking site, currently has 2.6 billion monthly users—222 million of whom live in the United States. A range of other platforms (e.g., Instagram, TikTok, Twitter, Pinterest, LinkedIn) serve niche populations and, in some cases, are growing so rapidly they have the potential to overtake Facebook's prominence in the United States in coming years.[3]

It is hard to guesstimate how many social media users self-identify as Christians. But, globally, it is surely less than a quarter. At our best, we show up in this space like the leaven Jesus talks about in Matthew 13:33—that teaspoon of yeast that affects the whole dough in a wildly disproportionate way. So often, though, it seems as if the contagion is working in the opposite direction. Christians on social media seem to be absorbing the meanness and deceit of the digital continent rather than transforming it. Our ways of pinging and dinging, tweeting and posting look a lot like those who have no relationship with Christ. Our online lives show no point of connection with Gospel values. Indeed, even in our discussion of faith-based topics (liturgical or doctrinal issues, social justice concerns, church news) we mirror all the sarcasm, reactivity, and wild swings that characterize a drunken bar brawl. We need to figure out ways to align *what* we believe about the God of Jesus Christ (God is Trinitarian Communion; God is Truth; God has become incarnate) with *how* we talk to one another. This book is an effort to do just that.

Social media is still a new form of communication in the history of humanity. (Facebook debuted in 2004. Twitter in 2006. Instagram in 2010. TikTok in 2017.) But Christian reflection on the purposes and practices of communication is not new. We could say that it began when the evangelist John penned the opening of his gospel—"In the beginning was the Word" (John 1:1)—and has been ongoing ever since. In the Catholic tradition, in particular, much of that recent reflection has found form in the papal addresses offered in advance of World Communications Day each year on the feast of St. Francis de Sales, the patron saint of writers. These addresses evidence one way Christian communities globally are trying to make sense of how to engage new media in light of faith.

In this book, I propose eight habits for Christians on social media emerging from the recent World Communications Day addresses of popes Benedict XVI and Francis, and suggest concrete ways to practice these behaviors in your own social media usage. At the end of the book, you'll be asked to sign on to these eight Christian habits. You'll also be asked to share the messages of this book to one other person and invite them to read it and sign on as well, becoming your accountability partner in this endeavor. One by one, two by two, in small, personal ways, we can transform the landscape of this new digital continent and make of it a place that God can call home.

1
#Clarify_Your_Purpose

While the speed with which the new technologies have evolved in terms of their efficiency and reliability is rightly a source of wonder, their popularity with users should not surprise us, as they respond to a fundamental desire of people to communicate and to relate to each other.... When we find ourselves drawn towards other people, when we want to know more about them and make ourselves known to them, we are responding to God's call—a call that is imprinted in our nature as beings created in the image and likeness of God, the God of communication and communion.

–Pope Benedict XVI, World Communications Day 2009

Have you ever caught yourself scrolling on your phone and had the fleeting thought, *What am I doing? And why?*

For me, there's a short answer to that question. Typically, I am a bit bored waiting for the next thing on my calendar, but don't have the time or mental energy to start anything substantial. I have a couple of minutes to kill. And in the immediate, it's an honest answer. But why do I even have social media accounts to begin with? Hmmm. It wasn't because I was thinking, *I have lots of time to waste. Let's see what more I could fill it up with.*

Rather, I think most of us—myself included—would say we got involved in social media because we want to be connected with friends and family, with people we no longer see all the time, with the wider world. We want to pass on information and learn about the things that affect us. We enjoy feeling we have a voice in the conversations of our time, and maybe can even have a bit of influence on those conversations. For some of us, there are additional economic, political, or philanthropic interests. We use social media to promote products, services, and causes that we value or that are tied to our livelihood.

Although it sounds a little strange to name aloud these underlying purposes, we should know that these are the same reasons why *any* form of communication exists. Linguists suspect that the earliest humans developed sign language to pass on information and work to achieve common goals. Humans adopted oral speech around 150,000 years ago, perhaps to free their hands for carrying and working with tools at the same time.[1] Around 5,500 years ago, our ancestors developed written language to expand the sharing of information across time. A little more than 2,500 years ago, the Persian emperor Cyrus the Great launched the first postal service to make possible the regular sharing of information across distances. Social media is simply another step in the long history of humans trying to connect more and more with one another.

God as Communion

As Christians, we understand this ongoing drive to connect is part of a larger divine plan. We believe that God is Trinity—a network of connection so tightly woven that God is three and one at the same time. God is divine "communion." And we believe God wants to share that Trinitarian life—by calling us always into community or the divine communion. In the opening pages of Genesis, we hear God say, "It is not good for the man to be alone" (Gn 2:18). God wants us to be in relationship with others and to become community with one another because that's how we learn what we need to share in God's own life.

Now brace yourself because this next idea is not an easy one to grasp, but it is important: *Communication is what makes community possible is what makes communion possible*. Sit with that for a moment and let it sink in, because that is what Pope Benedict wants to emphasize in the quote that begins this chapter. From a Christian point of view, the purpose of our words—expressed by way of gesture or speech, etched in stone or typed on a keyboard—is to create meaningful relationship with others, so that healthy community will emerge. And it is community that will help us realize God's plan for us.

The story of Babel from the book of Genesis gives us an example of what it looks like when this connection breaks down: Once upon a time there was a people who thought they could force their way into heaven by building a tower tall enough to knock on God's door. God halted their plan by confusing their communication, which fragmented and scattered their community. The story of Pentecost from the book of the Acts of the

Apostles gives us an example of what it looks like when this connection is restored: In the time after the Resurrection, there were people of many different languages who couldn't understand one another, but the Spirit swept through the city, enabling them to understand the words being spoken so that a new community made up of every nation could form. Communication, community, and communion with God cannot be separated from one another.

So, the fact that we are attracted to social media in those spare moments during our day (and maybe even more than that) is a sign of a deep and holy longing wired within us by God *for God*. Who'd have thought? Then, why does our experience online often look so much more like Babel than Pentecost?

Where Things Go Awry

Part of what contributes to the Babel-like nature of social media at present may be simply the newness of the medium. Our ancestors surely faced similar struggles when shifting from use of hand gestures to speech, or speech to written word. It took centuries, not years, to go from hammering the number of barley bundles on clay tablets to the evolution of an alphabet that could hold Sappho's poetry.

Many of our old aides to understanding do not work in social media: We can't read others' body language in the same way we can when talking in person or even on a video chat. We can't pick up the tone of voice behind a comment. It's easy to lose threads of conversation in the asynchronous back-and-forth. Without punctuation, hastily typed responses can come across sharper than we mean. Emojis . . . well, let's just leave that as a statement unto itself: emojis. All of which is to say that many of our struggles can be attributed to adjusting to what the current platforms can and cannot do in terms of helping us communicate with one another. For example, most of us know that Twitter is great for sharing news and not so great for facilitating deep and meaningful conversation on controversial issues. Over time, we'll figure out new norms and expectations that will make the platforms work for us better. We just aren't there yet.

But some of what plagues our communication on social media is what plagues all human communication. We *do* want relationship and community, but that's not all we want. We also want to be right. We want to be esteemed. We want to be funny and smart, attractive and influential. And even when we suffer doubt that we actually *are* these things, we still would like others to think of us that way.

These desires, like the desire for relationship and community, have always been with us, and they also are not bad. The problem is that social media fans these desires in powerful ways that can put them increasingly at odds with healthy relationship and community. Social media offers endless possibilities to project (or at least, attempt to project) a consistently funny, smart, attractive, popular, righteous digital self—and to do so in a very public way. At the same time, in the hidden space of our minds and hearts, social media offers endless possibilities to compare our real selves to others' digital selves.

When the selves projected online aren't the selves that we really are, the relationships we create online end up not being the relationships we think they are, and the online "community" that develops doesn't do for us what community is meant to do. Extensive engagement of social media has come to be associated with the following:

- FOMO (fear of missing out), a persistent sense of not being included
- lower self-esteem and sense of well-being in general
- increased depression and social anxiety, especially in youth
- poorer physical health
- lower reported life-satisfaction rating
- decreased face-to-face socialization with others
- decreased socialization with others outside one's own echo chamber
- lowered levels of compassion and empathy for others
- decreased civic/political engagement[2]

None of the above bode well for moving us in the direction of the life of communion God dreams for us.

So how do we reorient ourselves in the direction of Pentecost?

AN EXERCISE:
WRITING A SOCIAL MEDIA
PURPOSE STATEMENT

Writing a mission statement can sound grandiose and *sooo* 1988. It is not as if, for most of us, the transformation of the digital continent is our primary work in life. But when you think about engaging social media as a Christian, it's good to at least get clear in your own head about what you are doing on social media and why. And, if it helps, we can just call it a purpose statement.

Take a moment to reflect on your own reasons for engaging in social media. Make a list. What does being connected in this way do for you? In what way is your life richer for it? What relationship or community would you lose—or at least have less of a connection with—if you were not on Facebook, Twitter, and so on?

Think back to a particular moment or series of moments that were positive for you on social media. What was going on there? How could you have more of those moments? What do you hope will come about in the future as you engage in social media?

Reflecting on these questions will help you craft your own personal purpose statement for engaging in social media. Take a moment to write it down. It doesn't need to be long. In just a sentence or two, name for yourself why you are on social media—what you hope to gain by being on it and what effect you want to have on others online.

Showing up as a Christian on social media does not necessarily have anything to do with posting articles about your church or tweeting your love of Christ. That could certainly be part of your purpose statement, but it's not required. There are lots of other ways to evangelize, and lots of other reasons you might still want to engage social media. But showing up as a Christian online *does* mean that the reasons you engage align in a basic way with the reasons Christianity teaches any form of communication exists in the first place: to build stronger relationships and healthy, life-giving community.

Building relationship and community doesn't mean that we never say hard things to one another or that we never talk about politics. We need to be able to talk about the tough stuff in order for relationships to grow, and politics, by definition, is the art of trying to figure out the tough stuff so that we can live with one another in the best way possible. As such, politics can very much be part of one's Christian endeavor, including online. It certainly doesn't have to be part of one's social media presence any more than explicitly proclaiming Christ does, but it also isn't forbidden. If political engagement is part of your purpose statement, you'll just want to think about how to keep such posting aligned with your overarching goals for building relationship and community. We can certainly think more about that in the chapters to come.

For now, come up with a simple purpose statement for yourself. Here are a few real-life examples from Christian friends intended to get your own brain pumping:

> "I want to be on social media to remain in touch with friends who are not geographically nearby. I want to be updated on their goings-on and occasionally share something going on in my own life. I want to use Facebook as a format for sharing thoughtful articles and ideas, and occasionally as a place to ask questions and seek recommendations."

> "I want a space to take a stand on various issues important in our world today. I'd like to inspire others to see something in a new way and to join the fight for greater justice in society. I also hope to provide support and presence for people who I might not otherwise see in daily life."

"I am on Instagram to connect with people who have similar interests in baking. I am able to learn tips and share my own ideas—not just with people I know but with people who come from all over the world."

"I want to be on social media to encourage others and to help them see the light they are in the world. I also want to be a bridge to good resources, helping to share what is available on topics that mean a lot to me."

"I am on social media to connect with family and friends who live afar, and reconnect with family and friends I've not seen since childhood. I especially want to connect with other parents who have children with autism and to learn more about it. By what I post, I hope I can have some kind of positive impact on how people with autism should be treated."

"Grow my organization! I want to be on social media to share about the lives and cultures of others, teaching people to step outside their box and view life differently."

"Jesus said, 'The kingdom of God is at hand.' My goal is to post encouraging messages that empower others to see that goodness and beauty of God's kingdom/creation and the actions of others all around us. Sometimes that means sharing other uplifting posts, and sometimes it means sharing my insights and prayer artwork."

MY PERSONAL SOCIAL MEDIA
PURPOSE STATEMENT

_____

_____

_____

_____

_____

_____

_____

_____

Next: Am I for Real?

You have your social media purpose statement sitting in front of
you now. Excellent. But we aren't done with the exercise quite
yet.

Next, open the social media platforms you most engage,
focusing on those where you can fairly easily track your own
posts. When you look over your last month, or year, or five years
(I suppose it depends on how much you post!), what would you
say was the general intention behind your posting? Even if you
were not aware of it at the time, in retrospect, what would you

suspect the intention was? Perhaps you'll say that there was none at all, and that alone is worth paying attention to. My guess is that, as you scroll, a pattern will emerge. What do you see?

When you look at your posts in succession, would you say that your main purpose on social media seems to be informing others about what's going on in your life? Or about local issues? National or global issues? Is your intention to persuade others to get involved somehow in those issues? To vote differently? Is it simply to connect and keep in touch with family or a few close friends? To ask questions and seek input? Is it to market or support a particular cause? To share inspiration or express concern for those in need?

How does your observation of your own posts align with what you have named as your personal social media purpose statement? Are your efforts to reach out on social media allowing you to show up in the world the way you want to show up?

Do you spot things you've posted (or perhaps the way you've responded to someone else's post) that seems less than authentically you? Places where communication and community seem to be breaking down rather than getting stronger? Places where others seem to have misunderstood your intention in posting? If you are feeling particularly bold, ask a good friend or family member (someone you trust to be honest with you) to look over your main social media account and ask them, "If you did not know me in any other way than my Facebook page / Instagram profile, and so on, how would you describe me and what would you say was important to me?"

Take notes about what you observe—or what a trusted other observes—about your social media presence.

OBSERVATIONS

_____

_____

_____

_____

_____

_____

_____

_____

If your purpose statement for social media has nothing to do with building connection and community, you should step away from the keyboard: you are not yet ready to engage social media as a Christian. But in reviewing your feed, you should know that it is not uncommon to discover that even those of us who *do* want to strengthen relationship and community via social media find that we have shared things that run contrary to our overall purposes. That we are having impact on relationships and on our wider community that we don't necessarily want to have. That we are showing up online as someone not quite true to who we are or want to be.

It's okay. Christianity is about waking up to that reality and committing—with God's grace—to keep moving in the direction of becoming Pentecost people. That's what the rest of this book is all about.

Are you ready to commit to the first Christian habit for being and doing good online?

I will engage social media with increasing intentionality, striving to communicate in ways that strengthen relationships and build up healthy, life-giving community.

2
#Know_Your_Sources

We need to unmask what could be called the "snake-tactics" used by those who disguise themselves in order to strike at any time and place. This was the strategy employed by the "crafty serpent" in the Book of Genesis, who, at the dawn of humanity, created the first fake news, which began the tragic history of human sin.

–Pope Francis, World Communications Day 2018

Our own personal goal for social media may be to connect with friends and family at a distance, to promote healthy conversation, to share important information for building a better world. But we are trying to make those connections, foster those conversations, and share that information in the midst of platforms clogged with other feed that we do not control. Some of what shows up is news of the daily comings and goings of people we know, posted by people we know. Some of what appears comes from organizations that we've come to trust. And some of it comes from mysterious sources we've never heard of before and certainly didn't request to hear from.

One of the most troubling things about life on the digital continent at present is the proliferation of "fake news." Pope Francis defines this as "false information based on non-existent or distorted data meant to deceive and manipulate the reader . . . [often] to advance specific goals, influence political decisions, and serve economic interests."[1] This phenomenon should concern everyone, but in a most particular way it should concern Christians. Like "Trinity" from chapter 1, "Truth" is one of our most treasured ways of talking about God. We can say that we are committed to God only to the degree that we are committed to truth.

The Problem of Bots and Troll Farms

The 2016 US election and the investigations that followed made many Americans aware, perhaps for the first time, that much of the unsolicited content circulating in their feeds was generated not by legitimate news organizations or witty, well-intentioned friends of friends, but rather by bots and troll farms. Although the terms might still be unfamiliar and their meaning murky to you, you've no doubt seen their work.

A troll (which we will talk about more in chapter 5) is a person with antisocial tendencies who enters into social media discussions with inflammatory, provocative, or off-topic remarks for the sake of the personal enjoyment they receive from watching the resulting discord. A troll farm or troll factory, in contrast, is an organization that hires people to make similar comments or content for the sake of creating discord at a societal level, to fuel instability and influence political elections. Often the goal of the troll farm is *not* to persuade those who see their comments or content in a particular political direction, but rather to bolster and intensify what a viewer *already* believes to create a greater wedge between existing divides, increasing distrust and polarization. Troll farms author false stories that you'll be inclined to want to believe. They also share true stories, funny memes, and clever takes that will reinforce what you already hold. They arm you with great stuff you'll want to share with others, and they arm others with great stuff they'll want to share with you (which is most likely how it arrived in your feed in the first place).

A bot is an automated program intended to replicate human behavior online. Many bots are harmless and serve legitimate purposes—for example, the chatbot that your bank uses when you have a question. It isn't a real person that you are speaking to—and that might become incredibly frustrating at some point—but the bank's goal is to replicate a human interaction as closely as possible and point you in the right direction. Bots can also be used toward less honest ends, however. Bots can set up fake social media accounts and then create, like, and retweet posts in such a way that they manipulate the algorithms of the platforms, giving certain stories or quotes much greater visibility and credibility than they would otherwise have. Bots increase energy and interest around a story so that it is labeled as "trending," and, really, who wants to miss out on something that is trending? Who doesn't want to be in the know? A 2018 Pew Research Center report found that two-thirds of all tweeted links to popular news and current events websites on Twitter are generated by bots.[2] The study does not suggest that all of these bots are conveying fake news, but rather that bots are determining what gets identified as newsworthy in the first place and, hence, what makes it into your feed.

Content generated and disseminated by troll farms and bots can be difficult to identify and trace. Platforms have a number of ways for spotting fake accounts. They have coding, for example, to flag accounts that post or share more than one hundred times a day or accounts that tweet in multiple languages.[3] But even sophisticated coding intended to isolate bots can't catch all of them. Research estimates that between 9 and 15 percent of Twitter accounts and 5 percent of Facebook accounts are fake.[4] Moreover, it is extremely difficult to develop coding to identify fake news stories before they begin to be widely shared by real, live users. It is easier to stop a bot than to stop your old grade school classmate or your sweet neighbor down the street. The hard work of discerning whether a news story is true or not still lies primarily in the hands of the social media user.

Why Truth Matters

Sometimes when one of these stories is shared and a question is raised, you will hear people respond, "Well, it's true to me," or, "I'm just being honest about what I think." Honesty, or *truthfulness*, is certainly important. But saying whatever is on your mind and sharing whatever floats your boat is not what the Christian tradition has in mind when talking about truth. Truthfulness is about making sure that what comes out of your mouth is aligned with what is actually in your mind. But the value and virtue of truthfulness rests on something more foundational: having a mind that is aligned with reality. This classical

Christian definition of truth—articulated by St. Thomas Aquinas in the Middle Ages—implies that before we speak what is on our minds, we have to make sure that what's on our mind is an accurate representation of what *is*. We have to make sure that, to the best of our ability, what we share is factually correct and that the facts are not being manipulated selectively.

The Christian tradition often speaks of truth as "objective." One way of making sense of that claim is to say, "Reality is what it is." If we believe in "what isn't," things end up going badly—not for reality, but for us. For example, I may not *believe* in gravity, but if I step out of a fourth-story window, I will hit the ground at the same rate as someone who does. We can't make good judgments based on erroneous pictures of reality.

The objectivity of truth has implications for how we engage on social media as Christians. To the best of our capacity, we are obligated only to pass on news articles grounded in fact. Any opinion pieces we share need to use the facts responsibly (vs. manipulatively) in arriving at a given judgment. This can be tough to discern. As Pope Francis admits in his 2018 World Communications Day address, "The effectiveness of fake news is primarily due to its ability to *mimic* real news, to seem plausible. Secondly, this false but believable news is captious, inasmuch as it grasps people's attention by appealing to stereotypes and common social prejudices, and exploiting instantaneous emotions like anxiety, contempt, anger and frustration."[5] Nevertheless, the pope goes on, "None of us can feel exempted from the duty of countering these falsehoods."[6] If we share an article that turns out to be fake, whether or not we originated the lie we are participants in the lie and are to some degree morally culpable for keeping it alive.

How We Can Tell and What We Can Do

Because the issue of "doing truth" online is such a weighty one, let's talk first about what we should consider in reading and passing on a news story in relation to the story's factual nature. And then in the next chapter we can talk more about reading and sharing news stories and opinion pieces with concern to the question of bias.

The "news" is what many have called "the first rough draft of history."[7] It is the effort to tell the story of what is happening in our own time. In the race to tell that story as quickly as possible to keep people informed and help them to make good judgments, even the most truth-seeking reporters who are trying to be as objective as possible in their recording of the facts are going to give an incomplete picture. New information is going to emerge. Sometimes errors will be made. At the same time, there are tested structures and ethical guidelines that news organizations can put in place to demonstrate their commitment to objective reporting as best they can (e.g., hiring fact-checkers, being transparent about who is reporting the story and when there may be a conflict of interest, etc.). Some news sources adhere to these well-established practices more than others, and this is measurable.

When choosing what to read of the news stories that appear in your feed, choose stories from sources that are recognized for their commitment to honored journalistic practices. Wondering what news organizations that might include? Check out Ad Fontes Media (adfontesmedia.com)—originator of the helpful media bias chart. Or visit Media Bias / Fact Check (mediabiasfactcheck.com), where you can enter the names of over 2,900 global news providers and see how they compare. Both of these sources rate the factual accuracy of the reporting conducted by a news organization as well as indications of bias in the way they interpret the facts. News Guard (newsguardtech.com) is an online service you can link to your preferred search engine or social media feed that will flag stories from any source that does not meet minimal journalistic criteria. And, if there is a particular claim or statistic that comes across your feed and you want to check whether it is factually accurate, you can go to Snopes (snopes.com), Fact Check (factcheck.org), or Politifact (politifact.com).

Become aware of a couple of sources for news—not just one—that you can count on for trustworthy reporting, and read from these sources regularly to remain informed. (No one has enough time in their day to fact-check every story they read!) But do not give credence to stories from other sources, especially unfamiliar sources, before first checking them out. It would be better to scroll on by. And, certainly, do not share any stories from an unrecognized source. One of the most insidious tactics of troll farms is to pose as local news organizations. For example, neither the Kalamazoo Times nor the Ohio Capitol Journal are actual news organizations, though if their names appeared in your feed, wouldn't you think they were? At the close of 2019, approximately 10 percent of the most frequently liked and shared news stories in the United States came from sites that self-identify as news organizations but do not adhere to even minimal journalistic standards.[8]

If a friend shares a news story that you suspect may not be true, you have a couple of options. One is, again, to scroll on by and not respond at all to the post. Sometimes that may be all you have time for on any given day. A second option is to do a little research. Check, for example, on Snopes or Fact Check, and see if it has already been debunked. Copy the link from that site and let your friend or family member know. Consider whether it'd make sense to do this via private messaging rather than as a public response as a way of minimizing embarrassment. ("I saw your post about _____ and knew you'd want to see this link before the conversation about it online went any further.") If you see the story appearing in multiple places on your feed, consider starting a new post. ("Hey all, I've seen this story float-ing around a good bit online, so I checked it out on _____ and this is what I found out.") On some platforms you can also flag the story for the platform's internal monitors. On Facebook, for example, you can click on the top righthand corner of any post and report a post as problematic. One of the options you can select for why the post is problematic is fake news. Twitter has a similar feature allowing you to flag a post as "misleading about a political election."

AN EXERCISE:
HOW AM I DOING ON THE
TRUTH TEST?

Open up the social media platform where you post most frequently. Review your own posts from this past month or year, depending on how much you post. If you are someone who shares news stories (acknowledging that not all people use social media for this purpose), scan to see what the sources are of the stories that you've been sharing. Look up these sources on Media Bias / Fact Check (mediabiasfact.com). Does what you discover about the sources you've shared surprise you? Any trends you notice about the types of sources you draw upon most frequently?

Scan for news stories you've posted that arouse a lot of emotions for you. Stories that arouse strong emotions within us should serve as a red flag that the writer of the story might be trying to evoke a strong response from us, since we are more likely to share articles that we have a lot of feelings around. Pick a couple of stories to fact-check on one of the sites mentioned earlier (Snopes, Fact Check, or Politifact). Is the story you shared factually true? While you are on the site still, can you spot any other fake news stories that you remember seeing in your feed at some point but that have now been debunked?

OBSERVATIONS

_____

_____

_____

_____

_____

_____

_____

_____

If you discover that something you've posted is not true, don't beat yourself up over it. Know that it has happened to many of us on social media at some point in time. But, if the posting was recent—say, within the last couple months—let others know. Share what you've discovered, apologizing for having spread something you did not know was untrue at the time. ("I recently discovered that an article I posted last Thursday turns out to be untrue. Sorry to have fallen into the trap of fake news. Won't be posting stuff from _name-of-site_ again.") You admitting your mistake makes it safer for others to admit theirs and contributes to shifting the culture of social media. It offers a powerful witness to what it looks like to show up as a Christian online.

When you're ready, commit to the second Christian habit for being and doing good online:

> Before sharing a news story on social media, I will check to make sure it comes from a news source committed to sound journalistic standards. If there is a story that produces strong emotions for me, I will pause and check on its facticity before passing it on to others.

3
#Understand_Bias

The difficulty of unmasking and eliminating fake news is due also to the fact that many people interact in homogeneous digital environments impervious to differing perspectives and opinions. Disinformation thus thrives on the absence of healthy confrontation with other sources of information that could effectively challenge prejudices and generate constructive dialogue; instead, it risks turning people into unwilling accomplices in spreading biased and baseless ideas.

–Pope Francis, World Communications Day 2018

In the last chapter we talked about Christianity's age-old commitment to *objective* truth. Reality is what it is, we said. It's in our own best interest to make sure that our minds are aligned with what is, or we are in danger of making terrible judgments, harming both ourselves and others. Toward that end, we need to do everything possible to halt fake news—in other words, news that is factually incorrect or misleading. But there is a second way that we could understand Christianity's commitment to objective truth. Think for a moment of the list of "objectives" on the front page of a college syllabus or perhaps on the first slide of a PowerPoint presentation you've seen at work. Objectives give a sense of direction. They identify what we are striving for. In a similar sense, as Christians, truth always remains for us "an objective." It is something that we are constantly moving toward because, frankly, *reality is big*. While our brains can be aligned with it—that is, headed in the right direction—reality is never something that we would say that we master, even over the course of a long lifetime. As one of my colleagues is apt to say, reality is like a bazillion volts of electricity, and most of us are only dealing with 60-watt bulbs. We can know facts, but we can't know *all* the facts. So, while there are no such things as "alternative facts," we can acknowledge that there are always going to be *additional facts* that we are not aware of.

This second understanding of objective truth also has implications for our social media presence as Christians: We want to remain open to new information that expands our perspective and puts us in contact with the breadth, length, height, and depth of reality. We are not interested in entertaining false information, but we *are* interested in learning more true information and various ways of making sense of that true information so that we can live better lives.

The Challenge of Online "Echo Chambers"

One potential danger when we label stories as fake news is that we begin to use this designation not just for stories that are factually incorrect or misleading, but also for stories that we simply don't like. Stories that challenge the way we currently look at things. Stories that question the choices we've made. Presented with such stories, it is tempting to stop reading, even to unfollow or unfriend the people who post them. And sometimes, that might be the best option. (Again, one only has so much time in their day!) But in doing so we also lose the opportunity to learn things that might broaden our picture of reality. Worse, we could end up in an online "echo chamber"[1] where we are surrounded only by other voices who "echo" our views and reinforce them. As Pope Francis notes, disinformation ends up spreading rapidly in spaces where there is a lack of openness to additional information and a deep distrust of alternative perspectives.

Even without social media, we can find ourselves hanging out in fairly homogenous circles. We tend to live and socialize with people who are similar to us—in terms of race, religion, socioeconomic status, age, geographic location, and so on—and who naturally think in ways similar to us. The initial promise of the internet was that we would be able to connect with whole new groups of people from around the world and expand our thinking. This promise remains a possibility, but for many of us, the opposite has happened. We've ended up in online spaces even more homogenous than our physical neighborhoods.

Some have blamed the rise of online echo chambers on the social media platforms themselves for their role in creating "filter bubbles."[2] The algorithms that determine what we see in our newsfeed are designed to give us more of what we have liked in the past and to hear from the friends who we engage with most. In doing so, they filter out stories (and people) that—based on our past patterns of engagement—they think are not as interesting to us. Platforms could change their algorithms, and, indeed, experiments have already been conducted in showing more "cross-cutting" content to users (i.e., content from perspectives other than the reader's normal preference). But platforms cannot control who we choose as friends or who we choose to follow in the first place, and they can't control what stories we will actually click on to read. Studies indicate that even when feeds have a significant portion of cross-cutting content, users do not read this content,[3] and when they do, it is often only with the goal of reading for what is wrong with the story. Reading doesn't make them more understanding of the other perspective, only more infuriated.[4]

What We Can Do

By the time we are old enough to be on social media, we are old enough to have formed an impression of the world—both how it works and how we should live in it. This impression wasn't created in a vacuum. It began to form probably even before we were born. Some of the various ways that we react to the world may be rooted in differences in our brains.[5] A good deal surely has to do with our parents and the home in which we were raised. Our life experiences have shaped us in particular ways, as have our school systems, our communities of worship, our friend groups. The list could go on. And how good this is! Here, in the particularities of life, is where we learn our values. Here is where we come to faith. Here is where we acquire the wisdom of generations past. But here is also where we acquire bias—ways of looking at the world that predispose us to pay attention to some pieces of information and dismiss others. To pay attention to some people and dismiss others. To pay attention to some concerns and dismiss others. And often we are not even aware of the fact that we are doing so.

None of us can take in all the "reality" life has to offer. We can't read on every topic, explore every perspective, take on every cause. Remember, most of us are only working with "60-watt bulbs." And even if you are lucky enough to have been gifted with a 100-watt brain, in a bazillion-volt universe, the difference isn't all that great. At the same time, we want to be committed to mitigating the negative effects of bias as much as we are able. We want to leave enough space in our lives to look at reality from multiple perspectives and see if there isn't something of value for us beyond the beliefs that we hold at present. Something that might help us to become even more deeply aligned with the *truth* of things. At a minimum, we want to be open to anything that rids our lives of *dis*information.

Toward that end, we can be conscious of widening our friends group on social media to include persons we know to be quite different than ourselves in some way. We can follow news organizations and opinion page commentators who—while showing a commitment to factual accuracy—have a perspective on what the facts mean different than our own. We can then click on what they post rather than scroll past it, with an eye to learn rather than to react.

As noted in the last chapter, both Ad Fontes Media and Media Bias / Fact Check rate sources based on their factual accuracy and reporting bias. In pursuing truth as an objective, you are looking to read from sources that rate high in terms of factual reporting and close to "neutral" in terms of bias, with perhaps the addition of one source that would help to balance out the perspective you usually favor. (For example, if you realize you tend to read left-leaning sources, choose one that is known for leaning right.) Rid your media diet of sources that dwell on the bias extremes and those that rate low in terms of factual accuracy.

AN EXERCISE:
WHAT'S THE CIRCUMFERENCE OF MY SOURCES CIRCLE?

Open up the social media platform you visit most regularly and, to the degree that you are able, run some analytics. That is my fancy way of saying, let's take some notes: How many friends do you have? How many are you following? What do you notice about your social media circle? What kind of diversity exists in your circle? Do you have friends / people you are following from different parts of the country? The world? Do you have friends of different races, religions, generations, political perspectives? Is there anyone from your past or current life that you might want to friend or follow as a way of broadening the range of voices you listen to on a regular basis? Someone who you think might have an interesting perspective on life to share?

Then check the organizations, causes, and news sources that appear most regularly in your social media world or that you are following. Using the assistance of Media Bias / Fact Check, see if you can identify any bias generally associated with these groups. Can you identify a couple voices from a differing perspective that you might want to begin to follow as a way of expanding your own view? Again, you are not looking to read from sources that rate poorly in terms of factual accuracy or that are regarded as on the far right / far left of the political spectrum. You are looking for reputable sources that bring a perspective you would not otherwise have.

OBSERVATIONS

_____

_____

_____

_____

_____

_____

_____

_____

Committing to read more widely is *not* the same thing as committing to change your mind about anything. It isn't even a commitment to engage in conversation with others who think differently. But sometimes you might decide you want to, because conversation can be path to even more learning, even more truth—for you and for the other person. In the next couple chapters, we can begin to think about what good dialogue across difference looks like and what to consider before hitting the comment bubble.

When you are ready, commit to our third Christian habit for being and doing good online:

> I will strive to become aware of how my own bias limits who I interact with and what I read. I will widen the circle of people and sources that I engage on social media in order to put myself in contact with a broader reality than the one of which I am currently aware.

4
#Value_the_Person

An impeccable argument can indeed rest on undeniable facts, but if it is used to hurt another and to discredit that person in the eyes of others, however correct it may appear, it is not truthful.

–Pope Francis, World Communications Day 2018

Social media platforms are not built as digital bulletin boards meant only to provide information for those who scroll through their newsfeeds. They are built to get people talking to one another about what's been posted. They are built with space to comment and reply—not only to the person who initiated the post, but in response to others in their circle of friends or followers and beyond. A minute after you log on to social media, you can be in a rapid back-and-forth with someone you have never met before in rural Iowa. It's the coolest thing ever (a) most of the time, (b) some of the time, or (c) until it's not. Depending on who we end up conversing with on social media, we each probably have a slightly different end to that sentence.

One of the quirkiest things about social media is that you can get to know things about people that you would likely never have learned face-to-face: I followed you because I liked the books you wrote or the songs you sang, but now I find out that you knit sweaters for small dogs. That's interesting (albeit odd). And you love brussels sprouts. How amazing. I do, too. The more I read from you, the more real you become for me. The more complex and textured your personality.

But the opposite can also be true: The two of us grew up next to each other decades ago. I remember how one summer we played Monopoly every single afternoon, and you liked to be the boot. Me, the iron. You were good at math. You had an older brother who died in a car accident, and it was crushing. Your mom stopped showing up at church after that. But now I only see your head inside a circle on the screen, and sometimes not even that. I only see the hashtag-political-tagline that replaces your profile picture every other week. And I forget that you are a real person, not just a disembodied constellation of ideas. I forget that you have a spouse and kids who love you, though not perfectly. That you, like me, have good days and bad. That you, like me, have a whole range of feelings and still need compassion and understanding. But it is hard to remember all that, because the only you I have access to anymore is the digital you, which even on good days is still just a head.

God Became Incarnate . . . and That Matters

One of the core beliefs of Christianity is belief in the Incarnation. We believe that, for God, it was not enough to share with us only divine thoughts or teachings. God wanted to share in our whole lives. In Jesus, God took on not just a head, but a body. God took on our human feelings and desires, our physical sufferings and ailments. As Christians, we believe that, forevermore, every human life and every *aspect* of human life is imbued with divine dignity. We are called to respect one another and to relate to each other not just as heads but as whole people. That's not easy to do in everyday life. Even with colleagues I see in the office or family gathered around the dinner table, there are jabs made, humor that stings. There are times I treat the other as a means to an end, rather than the relationship as an end in itself. Times I see people as inconveniences, even problems, rather than as people.

Social media does not bring anything novel into the human struggle, but the lack of a physical, "incarnate" person in front of us does make it easier to slide into dehumanizing tendencies. In the banter back and forth online, with the absence of body language and eye contact it's easier to forget the realness of the person behind the post. And, hence, easier to treat the other without dignity. We feel free to say things, especially to strangers, that we would never say face-to-face.

The prevalence of fake news on social media discussed earlier further exacerbates the problem. More than a century before the internet existed, the Russian novelist Fyodor Dostoevsky observed in *The Brothers Karamazov*,

> A man who lies to himself and listens to his own lie comes to a point where he does not discern any truth either in himself or anywhere around him, and thus falls into disrespect towards himself and others. Not respecting anyone, he ceases to love, and having no love, he gives himself up to passions and coarse pleasures, in order to occupy and amuse himself.[1]

Yikes! Ever seen a better description of the comments section on YouTube? These are the reasons so many blogs, online journals, and news organizations—including Reuters, NPR, and Popular Science—have shut down the comments sections on their own websites.[2]

On social media, however, the ability to comment is, of course, baked into the platform. As we said earlier, it's why the platform itself exists. So, what to do then? How do we honor our belief in the dignity of the human person in the online back-and-forth? Perhaps it's best if we begin by talking about . . .

What to Avoid

Several years ago, when working on a project about how we handle conflict as Christians, I put a question out to my social media friends and followers asking if they knew of examples in the history of the church where we had "gotten it right." Where had we done a good job of handling tension in our midst? I was a bit dismayed to find that the most common response to my query involved St. Nicholas slapping the heretic Arius at the Council of Nicaea. Granted, most of my friends were offering the example tongue in cheek, and it was all done in good humor. But besides the fact that the story is historically false (and you know how I feel about fake news at this point), it says something that we are so short of stories about Christian-conflict-done-well that this is the first story that comes to mind. Even as Christians, when we meet someone who we are sure is wrong, our impulse is to want to attack the person, rather than the wrong.

On social media, the "slap" can happen in a variety of ways. It happens in ad hominem insults—when we dismiss what a person says not because of the content of their argument, but because of what we think about them as a person, often further reducing the whole complexity of their personhood to a simple label:

- "You would think that as a man."
- "Snowflake"
- "Such a boomer thing to say."
- "SJWs are always going on about . . ."
- "Right-wingers can't seem to . . ."
- "You liberals constantly fall prey to . . ."

Ad hominem attacks also happen when we only respond to what someone says and forget that there is a whole person behind the words who, even if wrong, is deserving of charity.

- "That idea's just stupid."
- "You've capitulated to leftist gobbledygook."
- "Anybody with a brain knows . . ."
- "Gauzy fairytale."

(Sadly, I did not make those examples up. All snatched from a fifteen-minute foray online.)

In Christianity there is an old maxim, "Error has no rights." We have no obligation to give something we know to be false equal airtime for the sake of providing "balance." But we want to stress that *people* still do have rights, no matter how wrongheaded their ideas may be.[3] They have a right to be treated with dignity,

with charity. That doesn't mean that we can't respond with con-
viction or passion or that we can't offer substantive critique of
ideas we find lacking. But tone matters.

The founders of the Harvard Negotiation Project, Roger
Fisher and William Ury, observe that we tend to think that in
order to be "hard" on a problem, we need to be "hard" on persons, or that in order to be "soft" on persons, we will also have
to be "soft" on the problem. Fisher and Ury argue that it is
possible to be "hard" on problems, while "soft" on people.[4] As
Christians, that is the approach that we are looking for. We want
to be courageous in calling people to be their best selves online,
to be responsible for their words and the stances they take. At
the same time, we want to do so in such a way that we show
care for them and seek to understand why they hold what they
hold rather than make fun of them. Research about what causes
people to change their minds on issues of substance indicates
that very few do, but when they do, it is only because they were
loved even in their state of error.[5] Being ridiculed or labeled only
makes people more entrenched in their perspectives. As indicated
by Pope Francis at the start of this chapter, if I have a deep and
abiding commitment to truth, I have to care about *being true* to
persons as much as I care about the truth of their words.

AN EXERCISE:
HOW HAVE I SHOWN THAT I VALUE THE PERSON?

Once again, scan through your most active social media account. Look for posts where you are expressing genuine care for another person. Maybe it is a reply to something hard that has happened in their life. (Those are the times when it is easy to express care, aren't they?) Scan to see if you can spot times when a person posted something that you disagreed with and you also managed to express care for their person in that situation as well. How was it different than when something bad had happened to them? How was it the same? What kinds of things did you try in order to communicate that you cared about them as a whole person, beyond only their thoughts and opinions?

See if you can then spot a post or two in your own feed where you think, "Oh, this conversation did not go so well." What was going on in that post? Are you able to spot any instances of ad hominem attacks in these posts—either on your part or others? Places where ideas were ridiculed rather than engaged? If you were to try to pick this conversation back up again, what would you do differently to tend to the relational aspect of the conversation better?

OBSERVATIONS

_____

_____

_____

_____

_____

_____

_____

Here we've been talking about what *not* to do, but in the next two chapters, we'll consider what *to* do—looking at ways of bringing up what we find problematic, while continuing to tend to the relational aspect of the conversation. It's important we find ways to honor the dignity of the other person . . . and our own dignity as well.

When you're ready, commit to the fourth Christian habit for being and doing good online:

In all my social media interactions I will remember that there is a real person behind whatever words and ideas are being put forth—a person who feels and struggles and has up and down days, just as I do. I will do everything I can to honor the human dignity of that person, even when I don't agree with them or their behavior.

5
#Lead_with_Curiosity

What is it, then, that helps us, in the digital environment, to grow
in humanity and mutual understanding? We need, for example, to
recover a certain sense of deliberateness and calm. This calls for time
and the ability to be silent and to listen. We need also to be patient
if we want to understand those who are different from us.

–Pope Francis, World Communications Day 2014

In the last chapter, we began to talk about habits we can form
related to discussion online, because social media is about more
than reading. It is about a certain back-and-forth—dare one even
hope, *conversation*—with one another.

Not all the time. We don't have time to comment on everything, even the stuff we like. So, we definitely don't have time to
comment on everything we don't. And if we do say something,
others may reply back. More time required. So, scrolling on by
is often the best we can do at any given moment. But it does
seem that if as Christians we want to have a voice in shaping
the landscape of the digital continent— "to grow in humanity
and mutual understanding," as Pope Francis says—then at least

45

some of the time we'll have to stick our necks out there and enter the fray. Ignoring *all* posts with which we disagree lessens our—and others'—chance of learning something new that might be important and helpful. The question is how to jump in.

When one of the first social networking sites, Friendster, chose the term *friend* way back in 2002 to describe the relationship its users would have with one another, it probably did not have in mind quite the same thing as Jesus at the Last Supper when he said, "I have called you friends" (Jn 15:15). Some (okay, including me) have complained that the way social media uses the term *friend* cheapens the meaning of the word. No one can maintain close, personal relationships with 692 people, some of whom they can't quite remember when they met. But Friendster's and Jesus' use of the term were also not unrelated. At its core, a friend is someone you approach with kindness and curiosity, someone you wish no harm and who you trust means you no harm. Maybe the use of the term can serve as a basic reminder how we are meant to jump into every interaction online.

In the fifth century, Augustine of Hippo famously penned, "nemo nisi per amicatium cognoscitur" — "No one learns except by friendship."[1] The saint was extending the concept of friendship here to the world of learning, noting that—beyond trying to understand other people—you can't understand even algebra, knitting, or Chinese grammar unless you approach your "subject" with good will, curious to ask the other questions and hear more from them. Just as you would a friend. But real questions are a bit of a rarity online, especially when one encounters a person or article with which one disagrees. More typical is the snappy adversarial tu quoque or "whataboutism" reply:

- "But your side also . . ."
- "I'll start caring about ____ when you start showing some concern for _____."
- "Well, what about . . . ?"

Can you think of a time when the discussion evolved from there into a great learning experience where worldviews expanded and human dignity felt honored?

Shifting the direction of an online discussion caught up in "whataboutism" feels about as easy as rerouting the orbit of the moon, but if I can remember to jump in as a friend would—curious, with a good question or two—sometimes I can still learn something new and we can "grow in mutual understanding." Even if neither of us changes our minds.

Questions That Work

Coming up with good questions that invite conversation rather than a free-for-all is not easy. A real question is not the same thing as a sentence with a question mark stuck on the end. ("Are you really crazy enough to believe that $%?") And any time we are asking a question that is trying to advocate our cause, to trap the other in their illogic, or to prove a point ("But don't you think that . . . ? Wouldn't you have to say that . . . ?"), we have not yet figured out how to approach the "subject" as a "friend." We are missing the requisite curiosity. A real question seeks information that the one asking *doesn't already have.*

If someone shares an article or expresses an opinion online and you are interested in having a conversation around it, lead with curiosity:

- "Tell me more about why you posted / why you responded. It sounds like this is important to you."
- "What do you think the author / I might be missing? What else should be getting our attention?"
- "Can you summarize what you heard the author / me say? I'm checking to see if we both heard the same thing."
- "What did you find to be the strongest points the author / I made?"
- "What kinds of experiences have shaped your own thinking on this?"
- "What would you be most concerned about if we headed in the direction this article is / I am proposing? What would be lost?"
- "If you were going to change your mind on this topic, what would you need to see to persuade you?"

If you decide to post something that you suspect might be controversial, you can prep for it becoming a learning conversation (vs. a verbal brawl) by framing in advance for readers why you've chosen to post on this topic and what kind of dialogue you are hoping it'll generate:[2]

- "Putting this out there because it is an issue I care about a lot and am always trying to learn more about. There are a couple things in what this reporter said that I was unaware of before, and I thought maybe you'd find them interesting, too. Anything you heard in here new to you also?"
- "I found this article valuable, though I realize it is a bit of a hot topic. I'd love to hear what you think about it. Please

don't reply until reading it all the way to the end . . . and no
ad hominem comments."
- "After reading this, I would be very curious to hear your
thoughts specifically around what we could do to improve
_____."

If you are not at all interested in having conversation with other
people about controversial topics, it is probably better not to post
articles on such topics in the first place. But it is also okay to not
want to talk about it on social media forever. Some professional
bloggers, for example, will say up front, "Two replies limit."

A larger question I often ponder is whether social media
platforms have the heft to serve as a container for the deeper,
complex conversations we need to have as a society and as a
church, even without any limits on the number of replies. The
conversations that we have on social media, especially when
engaged on our phones, tend to be asynchronous and brief by
nature. Twitter, in particular, limits posts to 280 characters. And
even then, the average tweet is 33 characters. Only 1 percent of
tweets hit the maximum number of characters.[3] The medium
appears designed for making announcements and a quick sense
of connection, but not for substantive conversation, especially
on controversial topics.

I have colleagues (almost always younger) who assure me
that you *can* have genuine learning conversations on Twitter.
That could be true. I just haven't seen it personally. I've read
things on social media that have broadened and nuanced my
perspective, but I've yet to enjoy a chain of replies with someone
on social media that led to substantially new and meaningful

understanding between us. Rather, the quick back-and-forth online provided the spark that led to a longer conversation outside social media. My own recommendation would be that if this is a topic you really want to explore more with someone, after two replies, pick up the phone or—better yet—continue the conversation in person. (And, yes, I realize this might be a generational preference!)

When to Ditch the Curiosity

There is an exception to this "lead with curiosity" rule: trolling behavior. You probably (hopefully) don't have any legit trolls among your actual social media friends. If you do, one would need to ask why. But if you scroll the comments section of any public page or follow any public figures, you have surely encountered trolling behavior.

A troll, as mentioned in chapter 2, is a person who intentionally injects disruptive comments into an online conversation for the sake of their own amusement, or what is sometimes referred to as "lulz." Trolls are more often men than women, and on psychological assessments they test higher in sadism, Machiavellianism, and psychopathy.[4] In essence, they derive enjoyment from seeing others upset. But not all trolling online is posted by those who regularly engage in it as a hobby. Many of us are prone to trolling-like behavior from time to time. When we are having a bad day and are exposed to comments of trolls online, we are susceptible to mirroring their comments in our own.[5]

In chapter 1, we talked about the purpose of communication being to build up community. Trolling does the opposite. It is communication turned against the very reason why communication exists. As in the case of fake news, there's no justification for it. It is sin. Never something Christians online should participate in, but tricky to figure out how to respond to. The best research at present says, "Don't feed the trolls."[6] Although it is hard, avoid responding altogether to trolling comments. In the words of comedian George Bernard Shaw, "I learned long ago, never to wrestle with a pig. You get dirty, and besides, the pig likes it."[7] Because the troll by definition is not interested in building up community but tearing it down, being curious and asking them questions to try and start a learning conversation only encourages further trolling behavior and gives the troll a forum for more people to see what they say.

The way that algorithms work on social media platforms, the more engagement a post gets, the higher it appears in others' newsfeed. A more effective response in such situations, then, would be to ignore troll-like comments and avoid posting further within that discussion thread. To refocus positive attention on an article or person you want to support, start a fresh thread, or share the original story again from your own account. If you yourself are being trolled, do not defend yourself online. Instead, block the troll immediately from your account. For additional steps that you can take, consult resources available from the Center for Countering Digital Hate.[8]

AN EXERCISE:
WHERE COULD I INJECT
CURIOSITY INTO MY SOCIAL
MEDIA CONVERSATIONS?

Once again, scan your own social media accounts, now with the goal of looking for the expression of curiosity in your online conversations. It may be difficult to revisit a series of back-and-forth comments on a public site, but perhaps you could search your own or a friend's feed for a time when you entered into a threaded discussion about an article or opinion that one of you had shared and disagreed upon. When you look at your own response now, how would you assess it? Were there any questions seeking more information, or were there only statements? Did the back-and-forth lead to a deeper understanding or relationship with that person or other respondents? Did it become an actual conversation? Did you learn anything that you didn't already know? Did anyone seem to change their mind or nuance their opinion? If you were to engage the discussion again, what kinds of questions would you want to ask to move it toward a space of greater curiosity and possible learning?

Perhaps it is not part of your own social media presence to post on controversial topics. But if it is, look for the last two or three times in which you did so. How were those posts received? Were they ignored? Commented upon? Liked but not commented upon? Shared? If you were hoping for real conversation, what might you have done in setting up the post to invite that? What would you like to experiment with next time?

OBSERVATIONS

_____

_____

_____

_____

_____

_____

_____

_____

Getting real conversation going on social media around complex topics is never going to be easy. But more and more it is the medium through which people are expressing their thoughts and feelings on these topics. Our challenge as Christians is how to move serial commenting in the direction of becoming genuine conversation where learning happens and relationships grow rather than stagnate. Like truth, friendship—even if only at the most rudimentary level—is an objective that we can always be striving toward.

When ready, commit to our fifth Christian habit for being and doing good online:

> When I come across something that I disagree with on social media, I will take a moment of pause to consider what I want my response to be. If I choose to engage, I will lead with curiosity to understand the other's stance better and see if there is something more for me to learn. If I choose to bring up a controversial topic myself, I will be open to conversation and learning more.

6
#Talk_about_Intent_and_ Impact

The best antidotes to falsehoods are not strategies, but people: people who are not greedy but ready to listen, people who make the effort to engage in sincere dialogue so that the truth can emerge; people who are attracted by goodness and take responsibility for how they use language.

–Pope Francis, World Communications Day 2018

I only meant it to be funny—this meme. This clip from late-night television. I only wanted people to be more informed with this commentary on the latest debacle in the White House. I was just remembering a great time. The awesome picture of the two of us smoking and clinking beer bottles in high school thirty years ago. Yes, I forgot that in tagging it, your sixteen-year-old would also see it.

But at the same time, you should know that sharing that photo of Chubby Me in a swimsuit at the age of twelve was inappropriate, Mom. Even if it is my birthday. And posting that

55

joke so soon after the tragedy was just tactless. And that opinion does not constitute an "alternative perspective to consider." A better description? Downright offensive.

It is one of the hard-learned lessons of life: We can have the best of intentions, but other people might not understand that. They will get angry, offended, outraged even. We wish they wouldn't, but they do. And then they blame us. There's not always much we can do about it.

But that hard-learned lesson has a corollary, easier to forget: When we are angered, offended, outraged, we are pretty sure the other person should have known better. Should have thought more about their actions in advance. Might have some sort of chronic character flaw—selfishness, ignorance, insensitivity, lack of boundaries. And we are pretty sure they *can* do something about it. Indeed, *should* have done something about it already.

The painful reality is that intent and impact are two distinct things. It is possible that we could have good intentions and still have a negative impact on other people. It is also possible that other people could have good intentions and still have a negative impact on us. Good intentions do not equate to good impact. Bad impact does not equate to bad intentions.[1] But when emotions are high, intent and impact get tangled, and it is hard to separate the two. Nowhere is this more true right now than on social media.

Ensnared in a System Larger Than Us

Intent and impact are tangled in every testy conversation. One of the most effective things we can do to defuse the tension is to take what communications experts call the "And Stance."[2] Allow the possibility that I didn't mean to hurt you *and* the possibility that you were hurt. Acknowledge you are offended *and* don't assume the other intended offense. Both can be true at the same time. Taking the "And Stance" doesn't fix the problem, but it does help to de-escalate emotion and bring one into a better space for talking things through.

When we are trying to talk through our different perspectives on social media, however, there are forces at work that would prefer to keep our emotions high. Heated emotion has long been a staple in the marketing diet. Anger sells. Not that we pull out our wallets and pay for things that make us mad. But anger focuses our attention and keeps our brain spinning on a given topic. On social media, anger keeps us engaged on the platform for longer periods of time. Research indicates that tweets, for example, that include "morally emotional" words—evil, diabolical, bans, punishes, hate, war, greed, shame, and so on—are retweeted 15–20 percent more frequently than tweets that don't. And tweets that include multiple morally emotional words can see an uptick of retweeting by 60–100 percent.[3]

Keeping emotion high serves the business model of celebrities and social media influencers[4] who can use their increased visibility to drive sales and brand recognition.[5] It serves the political strategy of some politicians who want to command constant attention, hopefully translating into votes in the next election (or deterring votes for the other side). And circulating content that keeps people engaged online longer serves the overarching financial success of social media platforms that rely on ad monies gleaned from greater viewership. Unfortunately, it doesn't serve social media users well, since it leaves us in an ongoing state of outrage that makes it harder to have fruitful online conversations.

Expressing outrage can create a sense of connection among those who experience it, and, occasionally, united expressions of outrage can produce specific changes. But rarely does expressing outrage change others' minds. And, strangely, the constant expression of outrage can lead to *less* social change. First, because we think that when we've expressed outrage or protested online, we've done something to correct a situation, but in reality there are far more effective ways of producing change (e.g., voting, writing elected officials, donating money, volunteering on the ground). And, second, because we can only be outraged by so many things before we become numb or find our energies so dissipated that our voice grows faint. In short, keeping us in a state of high emotion may serve the interests of a select few, but it does not serve what we as Christians would call "the common good." Relationships tethered primarily by anger don't lead to long-term healthy community.

So how do we break out of the cycle of outrage on social media to have more productive conversation with one another?

What We Can Do

The most obvious thing each of us could commit to as a Christian would be to not post stuff intended to anger or offend people. The problem is, unless you have some trolling tendencies, you probably are already doing that. You are sharing and commenting with good intentions. Granted, some might not have your sense of humor. Granted, occasionally you have a "hot take" that you think needs to be said to jolt people to their senses. But you aren't going out there intending to upset others. It's an unfortunate and, generally, unforeseen consequence. You didn't imagine others would get their knickers in a knot.

You are not off the hook, however. There is more we can hold ourselves accountable to as Christians. In the words of Pope Francis that began this chapter, we can commit to "take responsibility for how we use language." It's true that I can't control how others react to my posts, but I can still learn a great deal from their reactions. And if repeatedly I am getting feedback from others that I am posting stuff that is offensive to them, it's something to pay attention to. Yes, sometimes I do have a "hot take" that I feel needs to be said. Jesus himself had some of those. But if others are letting me know that they are experiencing what I say as not only untrue, but unloving . . . if what I am putting out into the world seems to be fragmenting community instead of serving the common good . . . then it is hard to argue that I am a Christlike figure here. There is another figure in the Bible that I am more likely giving witness to.

Speaking personally, I know I see myself as serious about the things people should be serious about, but also having a good sense of humor. I see myself as compassionate and caring about other people. If people on social media say something that puts any of those things in doubt, I'm likely to think that they are the problem, not me. They clearly just don't know or "get" me. But if repeatedly people are indicating they don't experience me as caring or appropriately serious, it gives me a clue that I'm not showing up in the digital world the way that I'd like to show up.

I'm not being seen in the way I'd like to be seen. And I should hear it as a call to ongoing conversion. I can choose to work to change my impact.

When any of us comes to such an awareness, one of the craziest things we can do on social media is to apologize. It's crazy because there is nothing about digital culture that encourages apologizing, and social media is not known for being a particularly forgiving place. But it is one way that we can show up distinctively Christian in a way that turns digital culture upside down, garnering a different sort of attention.

AND (remember that "And Stance"?) when someone else posts or responds in a way that makes me see red, I can pause and take a deep breath. If the person is trolling, I can do my part to stop the cycle of outrage by ignoring them and, where possible, blocking them from my feed. If the person is someone I know and want to stay in relationship with, I can choose to initiate further discussion that names impact and asks about intent:

- "Seeing this was a bit like a punch in the gut for me. Could you say more about why you retweeted it?"
- "I'm guessing that there was no offense intended. At the same time, I didn't find this meme funny in the current climate. Worried about how it might affect ____. Thoughts on that?"
- "When I read stuff like this, I get frightened about ____. I'm guessing it is not the same for you. Could you talk more about why you keep sharing articles on this topic? What are you hoping will come of doing so?"

Note that what we are doing here is building on the stance of curiosity we talked about in the last chapter, and taking it one step further. We are putting something of ourselves out there—how *we* feel, what *our own* concerns are—which can feel vulnerable. It's important to do this without judgment of the other or casting blame. We don't know what's motivating others. All we know is how it lands for us. But it can still be worth acknowledging that impact, even if the other person does not hear it in the moment.

A Word about "Good Humor"

Humor is a frequent cause of tension and hurt feelings on social media. Society has long struggled to distinguish between what constitutes "good humor" and what "crosses the line." It is challenging because no one entirely understands what makes something funny in the first place and why humor seems to be so culturally bound. (Russian jokes, for example, rarely produce laughter from Americans, whose jokes rarely produce laughter among Namibians.)

One theory of humor argues that laughter is a physiological response to an experience of the absurd when the absurd is experienced as benign. Let me try to say that more simply: We all have experiences (even on a daily basis) that surprise us by their oddity. Something happens that we did not expect to happen, and it takes a moment for our brain to figure out what is going on. If the surprise is one that our brain categorizes as nonthreatening to us, then the moment that we make sense of the unexpected, we get a little jolt of intellectual delight ("Hah!

I've figured it out!") that expresses itself as mirth. But if the brain does not perceive the unexpected experience as benign, the brain will not find it funny or delightful. Unexpected things that one finds threatening instead evoke anger or fear, preparing one to fight or flee. My suspicion is that the reason some of us experience particular political, cultural, or gender-based memes as good humor and some of us don't has to do with whether or not we experience the particular absurdity behind it as benign or in some way threatening.

Telling someone that they should not be offended, that there was no harm done, or that they are not being threatened increases rather than diminishes the experience of offense. A better response? Pay attention when others tell you your humor misses the mark with them. If it happens regularly, that is good information for you to have. If you are feeling courageous, ask about why. What do *they* think you might be missing?

AN EXERCISE: WHERE AM I ON THE OUTRAGE-O-METER?

Take time to scan through the last one hundred posts in your newsfeed. What percentage of these posts evoke some kind of emotional response within you? How many of them evoke some degree of anger or offense? 10 percent? 30 percent? 70 percent? Take note of what you observe.

When you look at angering or offending posts, are you inclined to want to ignore them or to say something?

What is the effect on you if you *do not* say anything? If you do not express your feelings? How will you mitigate that effect? Is there something meaningful you could do with your anger (e.g., call your congressional representative, donate to a cause, meditate, log out of social media, etc.)?

If you *do want* to say something in response, how could you reply in such a way that it moves the post in a constructive direction? What questions do you want to ask? How could you name the impact on you?

BONUS ROUND FOR THE EXTRA COURAGEOUS

Ask a friend or family member who you know will be honest with you to look at your social media account(s) with you and to identify posts you've made that might have come across as offensive to others, even if that was not your intent. Do they have one piece of coaching for you about the kinds of things to avoid in the future? Or about how to come across as the person you most want to show up as in the world?

OBSERVATIONS

_____

_____

_____

_____

_____

_____

_____

_____

When you're ready, commit to our sixth Christian habit for being and doing good online:

> I will avoid posting intentionally inflammatory content on social media for the sake of the common good. If something that I post offends people, I'll ask about the impact on them and take that into account in future choices about what to post. If something someone else posts offends me, I'll ask about their intentions and name the impact on me.

7
#Privilege_Face-to-Face_ Encounter

The new technologies allow people to meet each other beyond the confines of space and of their own culture, creating in this way an entirely new world of potential friendships. This is a great opportunity, but it also requires greater attention to and awareness of possible risks ... Does the danger exist that we may be less present to those whom we encounter in our everyday life? Is there is a risk of being more distracted because our attention is fragmented and absorbed in a world "other" than the one in which we live? Do we have time to reflect critically on our choices and to foster human relationships which are truly deep and lasting? It is important always to remember that virtual contact cannot and must not take the place of direct human contact with people at every level of our lives.

–Pope Benedict XVI, World Communications Day 2013

New Yorkers have long jested that Manhattan is the only place in the world where a pedestrian can get run over on the sidewalk by another pedestrian. But I suspect that nowadays the phenomenon is much more widespread. In recent years, I've been plowed into by people in any number of cities, and not just on the sidewalk. Indeed, I've probably done some of the plowing myself. The common denominator in these accidents: a phone in hand.

Our phones go with us everywhere. They vibrate multiple times an hour in our pockets. They are the first thing we reach for in the morning and the last surface our hands touch at night. They sit on our dinner tables alongside the knife and fork, as if just as important to our well-being as the food and family members before us. Research shows the meals we ingest with our phones present are less nourishing, relationally speaking. Eighty-two percent of adults surveyed admit that having phones present at a social gathering (such as a meal) "frequently or occasionally hurts the conversation." Yet 89 percent of the same people admit that they themselves used their phone at their most recent gathering with others.[1] Even if the phone never rings, its presence conveys, I am in your presence, but not fully in your presence. I am also available to a much wider social network with a multitude of other concerns and interests.[2]

Granted, people use their phones for much more than social media, and not all social media is accessed by phone. But the omnipresence of the phone serves as a symbol for the omnipresence of social media in our lives: We have a hard time being present to the people right in front of us when our attention is simultaneously coveted by 692 friends, 57 marketers, 4 political campaigns, 2 troll farms, and 1 potentially riveting video of a partridge in a pear tree. Not in the next room, but here on the table . . . closer than the salt shaker.

Why Face-to-Face Matters

In her groundbreaking work *Alone Together*, psychologist Sherry Turkle notes that whereas social technologies were originally conceived to help people who had existing relationships still communicate with one another when they *couldn't* be face-to-face, many of these technologies have now become preferred modes of communication, *replacing* face-to-face. As a result, the technologies allow us to be connected with more people, but in more controlled ways. We can opt in and out of conversations at will, on our own clock. We don't have to work to get together; we just click. Our connection can comprise just a couple of words and a smiley face. Turkle notes that such interactions are "friction-less." They require little personal investment or sacrifice. But in the end, they also only create weak ties. Having lots of weak tie relationships is fine and good and desirable. Such ties are of limited use, however, in helping us mature or in times of real need. Weak ties can't serve the same purposes that close friendships and family relationships historically have provided IRL (In Real Life).[3]

There has been pushback in recent years, even from Christian public figures who have a prominent social media presence, saying that purely online friendships should not be considered a lesser brand. That such friendships can be just as intimate and abiding as face-to-face friendships. Who's to say that online isn't real life if that is where we are spending so much of our time? Certainly, there are many saints in Christian history—starting with St. Paul—who built up relationships with those they loved primarily by letters rather than face-to-face.[4]

Some correspondence—for example between St. Francis de Sales and St. Jane de Chantal, or between St. Catherine of Siena and Bl. Raymond of Capua—testifies to a depth of sharing that many of us today would say we still only aspire to. But it strikes me that these very letters we are talking about always remained aspirational in nature: The saintly writers themselves saw the letters as a way of remaining in contact because circumstances prevented them from being together physically.[5] Or they saw them as stepping stones toward a future in-person encounter. To further an idea introduced earlier in this book, in the Christian tradition it is not just friendship, but face-to-face friendship that has always remained an "objective" worth striving for, even when it cannot be fully realized.

I suspect the ideal of face-to-face encounter has remained so strong in the Christian tradition because of our belief—again—in the Incarnation. God, too, it seems has always had a longing for physical encounter, a desire to draw closer and closer to us. Having a body still matters. And, while we might meet people online that we have never met before and occasionally might even strike up something that resembles friendship IRL, it seems to me we want to keep the "objective" of face-to-face friendship before us as a constant hope. Online friendship alone is "a bridge half built."[6]

Pope Francis conveys that sentiment strongly in his 2019 World Communications Day message:

> The use of the *social web* is complementary to an encounter in the flesh that comes alive through the body, heart, eyes, gaze, breath of the other. If the Net is used as an extension or expectation of such

an encounter, then the network . . . remains a resource for communion. If a family uses the Net to be more connected, to then meet
at table and look into each other's eyes, then it is a resource. If a
Church community coordinates its activity through the network,
and then celebrates the Eucharist together, then it is a resource. If
the Net becomes an opportunity to share stories and experiences
of beauty or suffering that are physically distant from us, in order
to pray together and together seek out the good to rediscover what
unites us, then it is a resource.[7]

For Francis, connection online is always an aid to something
more, never an end in itself.

What We Can Do

Ironically then, to live as a Christian *on* social media means
trying to move relationships *off* social media. Not every relationship and every interaction at every moment in time. Not till
heaven will we be able to enjoy deep and abiding relationships
with all. On this side of eternity, some ties will need to always
remain weak ones. But the relationships that we currently consider strong ties or would *like* to become strong ties cannot and
should not be relegated predominantly to the world of online
communication. Turkle notes that many of us show up in our
relationships as modern-day Goldilocks: "Not too close, not too
far, but at just the right distance . . . people who take comfort in
being in touch with a lot of people whom they also keep at bay."[8]

But strong tie relationships don't allow a convenient "just
right" that we get to control. Strong tie relationships require regular physical contact and—research is now highlighting—physical

touch. A hug. A brush of the shoulder.[9] Strong tie relationships are cemented by sacrifice and discomfort, awkward—indeed, sometimes painful—conversations and shared boredom. These relationships are not curated but cultivated, demanding time and quality of presence. In other words, step away from the phone.

For strong tie relationships we already enjoy, we need to invest time and energy to keep them strong because without ongoing effort, they will not stay that way. For online friendships that we'd like to *become* strong tie relationships, we'll need to figure out how to eventually move more of those interactions offline.

Unfortunately, in order to invest the time and energy needed to cultivate strong tie relationships, we will not be able to manage simultaneously an ever-growing number of weak tie relationships, if only because we are not God and do not currently have unlimited time and energy. University of Oxford anthropologist Robin Dunbar notes that historically humans have tended to spend about 60 percent of their day within a circle of the same fifty people (family, close friends and neighbors, work colleagues) and about 40 percent with people outside that circle (acquaintances, people in the marketplace and wider community). In the era of social media, that number appears to have flipped. But as Dunbar frankly observes, "The amount of social capital you have is pretty fixed . . . If you garner connections with more people you end up distributing your fixed amount of social capital more thinly so the average capital per person is lower."[10] Even though the amount of time it takes to like or comment is minimal, the time spent maintaining weak ties does add up when they are many. In the end, to give the relationships that matter most to us the time and energy they need, we may end up having to have the courage to let some relationships fade, trusting we'll see each other again in heaven.

AN EXERCISE:
WHERE IS THIS
RELATIONSHIP HEADED?

Get out a calculator, because you might need it for this exercise. Open each of your social media accounts one by one. How many friends or people that *you* follow do you have in each? What percentage of these people do you know and keep in contact with IRL beyond social media? What percentage of them would you say are strong tie relationships in your life? What percentage of them would you put in the weak tie category? What percentage of them would you put in the "no tie whatsoever" category?

For those you would currently consider strong ties IRL, how would you describe the impact that social media has had on those relationships over time? Has it deepened them? Made the contact you have with one another more regular than it would have otherwise been? Have you found yourself shifting more of the contact you would have had with one another to social technologies and away from face-to-face time?

Is there anyone currently in the weak tie or no tie category that you would like to develop a deeper relationship with? What ideas do you have about moving the forum for this friendship toward more face-to-face contact?

For profiles remaining in the weak tie or no tie bracket, how much time do you estimate every week you spend reading, liking, and commenting on content from this category? How much time do you want to spend? In chapter 3 of this book, we talked about expanding the circumference of our friendship or following circle to include a diverse range of voices expanding our understanding of the world and ability to look at things from multiple angles. Without losing the beauty of that breadth, it is important to also ask, Does it make sense to shrink the circumference of my circle so that I can give more attention to relationships I want to sustain or develop more? Some questions that might help in discerning an answer:

- Is this someone I know well or would like to know better IRL?
- Is this relationship and the content that they share "good" for me? In essence, am I learning something here? Do I like who I am when communicating with this person? Do I find myself regularly angry or "down" on myself or the world after reading what they share?
- If I stopped following this person's post, what would I lose from my life?

As an experiment, elect to unfollow or snooze for a period of thirty days those you do not know and do not see yourself developing a deeper relationship with unless you feel reading their material helps you to grow in some way and brings out the "good" in you. If you discover you've culled too much, you can always go back in a month and follow again, but see if the move produces any changes in your own well-being and, most especially, in the relationships that matter most to you.

OBSERVATIONS AND PERSONAL GOALS

_____

_____

_____

_____

_____

_____

_____

Dunbar's research indicates that historically humans have tended to have social networks of around one hundred and fifty people. One hundred and fifty seems to be the number of relationships a brain of our size can reasonably manage.[11] There is nothing sacrosanct or prescriptive about Dunbar's number, and human capacity can vary. It is only an average. But nowadays many of us have well in excess of three hundred social media friendships, sometimes overlapping with but often in addition to relationships IRL. At some point, something has to give. Let's just make sure it isn't the relationships we value most.

When you're ready, commit to our seventh Christian habit for being and doing good online:

> I will use social media to develop and deepen relationships that matter to me, keeping before me the ideal of face-to-face time with one another. I will avoid using social media in ways that dissipate my time and energies, leading to shallower communications across my life as a whole.

8
#Manage_Your_Energy

If the desire for virtual connectedness becomes obsessive, it may in fact function to isolate individuals from real social interaction while also disrupting the patterns of rest, silence and reflection that are necessary for healthy human development.

–Pope Benedict XVI, World Communications Day 2009

In the last couple chapters, we've identified ways social media can sometimes heighten tension in our relationships with others. But before closing, there is one more person Benedict and Francis are concerned about regarding social media, and that person is You.

"Who?" you ask. Yes, you read me right the first time: You. In practicing the social media habits you've agreed to, you've done such an amazing job reading and expanding your worldview, pursuing greater truth. Such an amazing job staying connected in relationships that matter and developing new friendships you'd never otherwise have had. Such an amazing job entering into hard conversations, asking good questions while remembering the human dignity of those you encounter. But in the midst of all this, have you also done an amazing job caring for yourself?

There is a subtle, almost hidden thread running all the way through this book, and it has to do with living inside the limits of time. In case you've not noticed it before, let me highlight it more boldly:

- "Become aware of a couple of sources for news—not just one—that you can count on for trustworthy reporting . . . (**No one has enough time in their day to fact-check every story they read!**)"—*Chapter 2*
- "If a friend shares a news story that you suspect may not be true, you have a couple of options. One is, again, to scroll on by and not respond at all to the post. **Sometimes that may be all you have time for on any given day**."—*Chapter 2*
- "Presented with such stories, it is tempting to stop reading . . . And sometimes, that might be the best option. (**Again, one only has so much time in their day!**)"—*Chapter 3*
- "It is about a certain back-and-forth—dare one even hope, *conversation*—with one another. Not all the time. **We don't have time to comment on everything**, even the stuff we like. So we definitely don't have time to comment on everything we don't."—*Chapter 5*
- "To live as a Christian on social media means trying to move relationships off social media. **Not every relationship and every interaction at every moment in time.** Not till heaven will we be able to enjoy deep and abiding relationships with all."—*Chapter 7*

Social media takes time. Engaging social media conscientiously will likely take even more time. And it's a sad fact of human existence: we are not blessed with an endless amount of it. Whether rich or poor, old or young, we all have exactly twenty-four hours to each day and seven days to each week. Furthermore, those activities in our lives that we find most nourishing—like learning, connecting with friends, and building up healthy, life-giving community—need additional time for digestion. Or, as Benedict XVI aptly implies at the start of this chapter, "Patterns of rest, silence and reflection" are "necessary for healthy human development." If some sort of equilibrium is not achieved, all the energy we put into showing up as a Christian online has the potential to negatively impact our well-being as a Christian offline.

How Much Time Do We Spend on Social Media?

Tracking social media engagement has become a preoccupation of both marketers and mental health professionals, albeit for different reasons. Current marketing research indicates that there are 2.6 billion people globally who engage Facebook, 1.4 billion of them daily. Facebook users spend an average of 58 minutes per day on the platform. Instagram and WhatsApp—both owned by Facebook—engage 500 million and 320 million daily users respectively. Instagram for an average of 53 minutes per day; WhatsApp for 28 minutes per day. While the world's 100 million daily Twitter users tend to spend only a couple of minutes a day on the platform, and Pinterest's 70 million daily users spend 14 minutes, Snapchat's 178 million daily users spend an average of 49.5 minutes and YouTube's 30 million daily users spend 40 minutes per day on these respective social media sites.[1]

Maybe that sounds like a lot. Maybe it doesn't. But hang on: it's important to note that most social media users have more than one account. Indeed, the current average is seven. So the typical social media user in the US presently spends two hours and six minutes daily on a platform. (If it is any consolation, this number is slightly below the global average of two hours and twenty-two minutes.)[2] Looking at the data from another perspective: if you live the average global human life span of seventy-two years and engage social media at 2020 rates, you will spend six years and eight months of your life on social media (in comparison to three years and seven months eating and drinking).[3] And if that doesn't startle you, consider that there are others who will spend more. Much more.

Social Media Addiction and Obsession

There is growing concern in the mental health community regarding the possibility of social media addiction. While not officially listed in the *Diagnostic and Statistical Manual of Mental Disorders, Fifth Edition,* there are a number of studies indicating that "the brain on social media" can look a lot like "the brain on drugs." Heavy social media users begin to exhibit the same characteristics as persons with other substance abuse disorders, including the following:

- compulsory behavior ("I *have* to check online")
- mood changes ("My mood improves when I check in; gets worse when I can't")
- tolerance ("I need to check in more frequently / longer in order to get the same degree of satisfaction I had in the past")

- impact on quality of life ("I am having a hard time holding down my job, maintaining important relationships, getting enough sleep")
- dishonesty ("I am lying to myself and/or others about the amount of time I'm spending online")
- relapse ("I tried to minimize / cut off my use of social media, but found myself in the same patterns of use again")

Researchers who study addiction have looked at how social media can cause a rise in dopamine levels in the brain. Dopamine is an organic chemical associated both with pleasure and "motivational salience." In essence, dopamine gives you an emotional buzz and motivates you to do what's needed to get more of that buzz. We naturally experience a dopamine bump in relationships when we share about ourselves and are affirmed by others. That's good! It's how we are wired as humans. But social media "turns up the volume" on that natural phenomenon, offering *endless* opportunity to share about ourselves[4] and get likes. In order to feel the same buzz, we end up needing more and more likes, and we keep checking for them more and more frequently. Notifications from social media platforms—both the little red circle on the corner of the phone app and the repeated vibration when someone responds—function in a similar manner as the bell for Pavlov's dogs: we get excited that something tasty is coming our way.[5]

Other researchers have focused more on how social media use can raise levels of cortisol and adrenaline in the brain. Unlike dopamine, cortisol and adrenaline are organic chemicals associated with "fight or flight." (In essence, they tell you, "Be alert! Something important for your survival and thriving is at stake here, so pay attention because you may need to move quickly!") Because we fear missing out on what important thing might be happening online (with friends, in the news, etc.), we experience a cortisol- and adrenaline-induced anxiety and "jumpiness" when we are not on social media which is only alleviated by checking in online. Notifications from social media platforms feed the fear that we are missing something, ratcheting up the tension. Rather than framing social media as addictive, these researchers emphasize the danger of social media *obsession*: compulsive behavior driven not by pleasure but anxiety.[6]

About 5–10 percent of Americans fully exhibit the markers of a social media addiction as described above, but many more will recognize, "Hmm. I think at least some of these markers are true of me . . . at least occasionally." Indeed, in a 2019 survey 40 percent of respondents admitted "feeling addicted" some or all of the time.[7] So, whether what we suffer is a true addiction, a dependency, or an obsession, what's being described is an experience of loss of human freedom, which as Christians we should care about a great deal.

A core doctrine of Christianity is that we were created with free will. God is free and makes *us* free because we need freedom in order to truly enjoy that Trinitarian life, the life of communion, we are meant for, as described in chapter 1. This life is one of friendship with God, who by very nature *is* Friendship. And friendship by definition is a relationship freely entered into. (If you found out someone was being paid to be your friend, how would you feel?) So, anything that diminishes our freedom, anything that smacks of compulsion—like addiction or obsession—is problematic, not only for physical or emotional well-being, but for spiritual well-being. It harms our capacity to live the lives God has created us to live and pursue the end God has intended us to pursue.

What Can We Do

In his widely read classic *The Sabbath,* Jewish rabbi Abraham Heschel describes how we as humans are prone to work ourselves into a frenzy of activity, in part because we don't know what to do with the mystery of time. Time, as noted earlier, is the one thing we can't control. The world of space, of things—we have the ability to impact. But time? No matter what we do, we can't make it move faster or slower. Time is where we encounter our limits, because ultimately, Heschel observes, time belongs exclusively to God.[8] The question isn't how to manage *time* better, but how to manage *ourselves* better *in time.* How to live human freedom within our human limits. What can help?

A number of well-established recommendations relate to phone usage. Research indicates that 78 percent of social media users log in exclusively by phone. Another 20 percent sometimes also use their computers or tablets, but only 1.8 percent of users engage exclusively by computer or tablet.[9] This data seems to indicate that if we could better manage ourselves on our phones, we'd make great headway in reigning in compulsive social media tendencies. Ideas?

- *Turn off all screen notifications*—This simple adjustment will decrease both the pleasurable intrigue and the anxiety that drive the desire to check social media constantly.

- *Keep only tools on your front screen*—We go onto our phones to check a contact, the weather, or get directions, and without knowing it suddenly find ourselves checking Instagram. Moving all social media apps to the second or third screen, so that you have to scroll to get to them, keeps you from being tempted whenever you pick up your phone.
- *Go to gray screen*—Bright colors are like candy for our eyes. Changing your screen to gray scale or monochrome within your phone's settings often decreases the amount of time spent on your phone.[10]
- *Charge your phone outside of your bedroom*—When the phone is right next to your bed, it is easy to check it one last time before going to sleep or first thing in the morning. The fact that you are in a comfortable, warm space makes it even more tempting to stay put for longer.
- *Download an app to help*—Apps exist that can delay the opening of social media when you click on it, forcing you to pause and ask, "Is this really what I want to be doing right now?" Other apps can lock you out of the platform after a certain period of time that you decide upon. Besides the features already present on most phones, popular options include Freedom, AppBlock, Moment, and KeepMeOut.
- *Remove social media from your phone*—It is the most radical of the options, but clearly also the most effective. Only allow yourself access from your computer.

Other common recommendations relate to our devices in general:

- *Have set times for social media*—There is no rule establishing the number of minutes per day or week Christians should limit themselves to on social media. We are using it for such varied purposes! But each of us should reflect on how much time we *want* to dedicate to social media and then hold ourselves to it. Having a set time of day or a set day of the week that you know you will check in helps to establish boundaries on usage. Setting a timer reminds not to go beyond those boundaries.

- *Turn off all devices one hour before going to bed*—Beyond the fact that social media can rob us of time we might otherwise use for sleep, the devices used to access social media are themselves detrimental to good sleep. The blue light emitted by electronic screens suppresses the natural release of melatonin—another important chemical in the brain regulating the body's internal clock.

- *Practice "Tech Shabbat"*[11]—"Tech Shabbat" is a modern adaptation of the age-old biblical practice of Sabbath that Heschel writes about, increasingly popular in both Jewish and Christian communities. It involves a commitment to set aside one full day a week to being offline: no social media, no email, no texting, no online gaming, no web surfing. In the Jewish community, this day aligns with the weekly Shabbat from sundown on Friday to sundown on Saturday. But if that timeframe doesn't work for you right now, choose another that would. And if eliminating all technology feels too overwhelming at present, begin with a social-media-only-free-day, and see where things evolve from there. Start with what you can do, and don't allow the ideal to become the enemy of the possible.

AN EXERCISE:
HOW MUCH TIME DO I SPEND? HOW MUCH TIME DO I WANT TO SPEND?

Ready for one last exercise? Believe it or not, this one does not involve scrolling through your social media newsfeed, but rather going into the settings of your phone and/or your social media apps. The specifics of how you might do this vary from device to device, but—perhaps with the extra step of googling for advice as to how—find out how much screen time you have averaged per day this week on your phone. One click further should allow you to see how much time you have spent on social networking apps in particular. Some apps (e.g., Facetime or Instagram) allow you to also go into their settings to find out how much time you've spent specifically in their app over the past seven days. (This opportunity, at the point of publication, is only available through the phone app and does not track computer usage of the platform.)

Does what you've discovered surprise you? Does the number of hours and minutes seem about right to you? Is it more or less than you thought it would be? How do you feel about this number? Is it one that makes sense for your life right now?

Given your purposes for being on social media, what would you consider to be an ideal amount of time each day or week to spend on the platforms you are a part of? Knowing yourself, do you see it as better to do short, frequent check-ins? Or would it be better for your health and well-being to have set times to check in? What is your rationale?

OBSERVATIONS AND PERSONAL GOALS

_____

_____

_____

_____

_____

_____

_____

_____

NEXT:
LET'S TRY THIS OUT

Having decided how much time you *want* to spend on social media each day or week, turn toward action. Is there a particular strategy you want to test this week to keep yourself within the boundaries you've set?

Carefully monitor your social media usage during the coming week using tools available on your phone (or a simple timer). At the end of the week, assess your efforts. Were you able to stay within the time you'd allotted for yourself? Is there anything new you'd want to try?[12]

OBSERVATIONS

_____

_____

_____

_____

_____

_____

_____

If you find that your use of social media during this period continues to exceed the amount of time you set, monitor again for another couple of weeks, trying some of the other tips from this chapter. If after a month you find yourself still not able to stay within your target, bring a friend, spouse, or other family member on board to help hold you accountable. When we make a commitment aloud, we tend to follow through on it more. And if that doesn't work, consider getting additional assistance. There are a growing number of counseling resources available to those struggling with overuse of the internet in general, and talking to a professional might be key to managing yourself better in the mystery of time.

And now, when you're ready, it's time to commit to our eighth and final Christian habit for being and doing good online:

> I will monitor my use of social media to make sure that the time I spend online makes sense for my own health and well-being, allowing for "the patterns of rest, silence and reflection that are necessary for healthy human development."

Epilogue

I have been on social media now for about ten years. I jumped into it without a great deal of forethought. I was mildly intrigued, if hesitant, when a good friend asked me, "Do you like to get Christmas cards?"

"Yes, helps me know people are still alive," I said.

"Do you especially like it when the person writes a bit of what they are up to?" she asked.

"Definitely," I replied.

"Then you should try Facebook," she said.

Hah. Ten years later, my friend who became my first "friend" rarely accesses the platform, and I've become one of those people who spends an average of fifty-eight minutes a day there. Apparently, some of us enjoy the holidays more than others. I also make occasional forays onto Twitter, LinkedIn, Pinterest, and YouTube. I hope not two hours and six minutes per day, but that is probably not unheard of.

Over the course of the past ten years, I suspect I've violated every Christian habit espoused in this book. I imagine I've shared fake news unsuspectingly. I know there are some news sources I regularly bias that are themselves biased. I'm sure I've been guilty of an ad hominem comment or two or twenty. I've avoided or shut down conversations I could (should?) have pursued. I've neglected to ask questions and neglected to share impact. I've checked my phone at the dinner table while berating my husband for doing the same. I've scrolled social media while on conference calls. I've told myself, "I need to cut back," then found myself unwittingly online again.

But I like to think I'm getting better (if only by the grace of God) because I am waking up more and more to the way in which my online presence is a reflection of my identity as a Christian. Christianity is about more than assenting to a certain set of statements regarding God. It is about the way you show up in the world. And it is not about just showing up that way on Sundays. Our faith is meant to permeate every part of our lives every day of the week. You cannot believe that God is Truth and be complicit in sharing false or highly biased stories. You cannot believe that God became incarnate in the person of Jesus Christ and disrespect human dignity in the comments_section. And you cannot believe that God is Trinity—that God in God's very being is Friendship—and not care about having healthy friendships yourself. Or about the building up of healthy community.

The writings of popes Benedict and Francis in their annual World Communications Day messages have illuminated these points consistently and have been a source of inspiration for me and for many. Amidst all negativity surrounding social media in recent years, the popes have persistently conveyed a positive vision of what life on the "digital continent" could be if engaged with virtue. They've given me hope. I doubt that hope could have been sustained, however, without the daily witness of many social media friends who showed me what the popes' vision looked like in practice.

I have a few friends who've been exceptional in this regard. They regularly share interesting, well-chosen articles. They invite conversation. They ask good questions. They distinguish between intent and impact. Sometimes they change their minds. They apologize when needed. These friends post about their own lives while maintaining healthy boundaries. They don't share everything, but what they do share reflects who they really are . . . no false pretenses. Because of the way that they show up in social media, I know more than I would otherwise—about them and about the world. I feel more connected to them. More informed about the world. And I do taste a hint of God's friendship in their friendship. They represent social media at its best for me. A sign of the kind of social media user I aspire—no, commit—to become.

I hope that you also have some social media friends like that. And, if you've read thus far, I hope you also share a similar commitment. I invite you to sign on to the Christian habits for online behavior that we've explored in this book (a complete list is found at the end of this book). I suggest you ask a fellow social media friend to sign on with you so that you have a partner in making sure these habits do not go unpracticed. Choose a person you trust. Someone who cares about you being your best self and who will let you know—maybe by a secret emoji signal the two of you decide upon—when you are not showing up that way online. Finally, I invite you to sign your name to the #Rules_of_Engagement at anngarrido.com/rules as a way of making your commitment public. There, I let you know my own "secret" emoji signal and invite you to use it if you see *me* show up as less than my best digital self. I want you to include next to it the number of the habit you see me needing better to hold myself accountable to. All of us—including me—need to count on each other to help us live our Christian faith online as robustly as we are able.

A Pause for Prayer

Throughout this book, we've experimented with a number of exercises. Let's close instead with a prayer. Spend a couple of minutes on your favored social media accounts scanning for the names of friends or those you follow who have modeled for you the living of these eight habits—whether they knew that was what they were doing or not. Perhaps you might have a different name in mind for each of the eight. Perhaps you find there are a few people in your social media circle who seem to embody the whole list. Write up to eight names in the space below.

NAMES OF "MODEL FRIENDS"

_____

_____

_____

_____

_____

_____

_____

_____

Spend a couple moments thanking God for their presence in your life. Speak to God about what you admire in each of them and ask God's grace to be able to emulate a similar quality of presence on social media. Then, using Pope Francis's prayer offered at World Communications Day 2018, bow your head in prayer—for yourself, for those you've named, and for all of us committed to showing up as our best digital selves:

> Lord, make us instruments of your peace.
> Help us to recognize the evil latent in a communication that does not build communion.
> Help us to remove the venom from our judgments.
> Help us to speak about others as our brothers and sisters.
> You are faithful and trustworthy; may our words be seeds of goodness for the world:
> where there is shouting, let us practice listening;
> where there is confusion, let us inspire harmony;
> where there is ambiguity, let us bring clarity;
> where there is exclusion, let us offer solidarity;
> where there is sensationalism, let us use sobriety;

where there is superficiality, let us raise real questions;
where there is prejudice, let us awaken trust;
where there is hostility, let us bring respect;
where there is falsehood, let us bring truth.
Amen.[1]

Thank You

The idea behind the eight habits is not my own. It belongs to IRL friend, social media friend, and (not coincidentally) long-time editor Eileen Ponder. Out of our own experiences on social media—which were both deeply concerning and hopeful—we began to bat around the idea of collaborating on a project offering a faith perspective on online behavior. What you should also know is that Eileen is one of those people who appears on *my* list of model friends from the epilogue. She is as thought-provoking and funny online as she is offline. I am always learning from what she posts.

Also on that list of model friends are a couple of people who have no clue what a good influence they have been on me. There are many well-known Christian folk I follow who I think do social media with a lot of integrity. But I'd like to thank a few "ordinary" folks—among many—who are doing an extraordinarily good job doing all the things talked about in this book, including regularly opening up tough political and ecclesial conversations: Dan Frachey, Shelley Finkler, Orin Johnson, Unni Berkes, Matthew Irwin, Sarah Lindamood. I've learned a lot by watching how they handle diverse perspectives with grace.

I am soooo grateful for friends and followers who've taken the time to reply to all my crazy requests for input on this project over the course of the past year—sharing with me your reasons for being on social media in the first place and how your life is different for it. A particularly treasured thought partner has been my son, Micah, who—being a millennial—was born with an innate knowledge regarding social media that I am still acquiring. He has been schooling me since the age of fourteen, when he posted this sage advice: "Mom, I can see who you are. You don't need to sign your wall posts." Also to be thanked: my husband, Miguet, who has a checkered history on social media. On. Off. On. Off. But is currently back on, possibly with the main goal of making Micah roll his eyes. And, last but not least, Sheila "it's-like-getting-Christmas-cards" Heen who first got me up on social media. Christmas cards? Seriously.

Appendix:
Eight Christian Habits on Social Media

Publicly share your commitment by signing the #Rules_of_ Engagement pledge at anngarrido.com/rules or by scanning the QR code below. After adding your signature, tell a friend about this book. Ask your friend to read and sign on as well. Become partners in holding each other accountable in living the eight habits.

1. I will engage social media with increasing intentionality, striving to communicate in ways that strengthen relationships and build up healthy, life-giving community.

2. Before sharing a news story on social media, I will check to make sure it comes from a news source committed to sound journalistic standards. If there is a story that produces strong emotions for me, I will pause and check on its facticity before passing it on to others.

3. I will strive to become aware of how my own bias limits who I interact with and what I read. I will widen the circle of people and sources that I engage on social media in order to put myself in contact with a broader reality than the one of which I am currently aware.

4. In all my social media interactions I will remember that there is a real person behind whatever words and ideas are being put forth—a person who feels and struggles and has up and down days, just as I do. I will do everything I can to honor the human dignity of that person, even when I don't agree with them or their behavior.

5. When I come across something that I disagree with on social media, I will take a moment of pause to consider what I want my response to be. If I choose to engage, I will lead with curiosity to understand the other's stance better and see if there is something more for me to learn. If I choose to bring up a controversial topic myself, I will be open to conversation and learning more.

6. I will avoid posting intentionally inflammatory content on social media for the sake of the common good. If something that I post offends people, I'll ask about the impact on them

and take that into account in future choices about what to post. If something someone else posts offends me, I'll ask about their intentions and name the impact on me.

7. I will use social media to develop and deepen relationships that matter to me, keeping before me the ideal of face-to-face time with one another. I will avoid using social media in ways that dissipate my time and energies, leading to shallower communications across my life as a whole.

8. I will monitor my use of social media to make sure that the time I spend online makes sense for my own health and well-being, allowing for "the patterns of rest, silence and reflection that are necessary for healthy human development."

Signature: _____

Date: _____

Accountability Partner Name/Signature:

_____

Notes

Introduction

1. A fair question at this point: What do you mean by social media? Working from a set of markers established at https://historycooperative.org/the-history-of-social-media/, in this book I define social media as online (i.e., internet-based) communication that is user generated. Websites and blogs are not included because a limited number of people are able to post to these sites, so content is not broadly user generated. Profile-based platforms (e.g., Facebook, Twitter, LinkedIn), messaging services (e.g., WhatsApp), and video portals (e.g., YouTube) would be included under this criteria. Throughout this book I'll focus primarily on profile-based platforms.

2. Benedict XVI, "Message of His Holiness Pope Benedict XVI for the 43rd World Communications Day," *Libreria Editrice Vaticana*, January 24, 2009, http://www.vatican.va/content/benedict-xvi/en/messages/communications/documents/hf_ben-xvi_mes_20090124_43rd-world-communications-day.html.

3. Current statistics on Facebook are available at https://about.fb.com/company-info/. A summary of 2020 Q1 statistics (from which the numbers in the text are based) can be found

at https://zephoria.com/top-15-valuable-facebook-statistics/. For numbers specifically related to US users, see https://www. statista.com/statistics/408971/number-of-us-facebook-users/. Helpful general information about social media in the United States can be found at https://www.pewresearch.org/internet/ fact-sheet/social-media/.

1. Clarify Your Purpose

1. Colin McGinn, *Prehension: The Hand and the Emergence of Humanity* (Cambridge, MA: MIT Press, 2015), accessed via e-book.

2. The literature on the negative impact of social media is extensive. Research that I consulted includes Bridget Dibb, "Social Media Use and Perception of Physical Health," accessed through the National Institutes of Health, https://www.ncbi. nlm.nih.gov/pmc/articles/PMC6327064/; Igor Pantic, "Online Social Networking and Mental Health," accessed through the National Institutes of Health, https://www.ncbi.nlm.nih.gov/ pmc/articles/PMC4183915/; Eitan Hersh, *Politics Is for Power: How to Move Beyond Political Hobbyism, Take Action, and Make Real Change* (New York: Simon and Schuster, 2020); Hunt All-cott, Luca Braghieri, Sarah Eichmeyer, and Matthew Gentzkow, "The Welfare Effects of Social Media," available at https://web. stanford.edu/~gentzkow/research/facebook.pdf.

2. Know Your Sources

1. Pope Francis, "Message of His Holiness Pope Francis for World Communications Day," Libreria Editrice Vaticana,

January 24, 2018, http://www.vatican.va/content/frances-co/en/messages/communications/documents/papa-frances-co_20180124_messaggio-comunicazioni-sociali.html.

2. Stefan Wojcik, Solomon Messing, Aaron Smith, Lee Rainie, and Paul Hitlin, "Bots in the Twittersphere," Pew Research Center, April 9, 2018, https://www.pewresearch.org/twitterbots.

3. For additional information on ways to identify bots, see Carlotta Dotto and Seb Cubbon, "How to Spot a Bot (or Not): The Main Indicators of Online Automation, Co-Ordination and Inauthentic Activity," First Draft, November 28, 2019, https://firstdraftnews.org/latest/how-to-spot-a-bot-or-not-the-main-indicators-of-online-automation-co-ordination-and-inauthen-tic-activity/.

4. Onur Varol, Emilio Ferrara, Clayton A. Davis, Fillippo Menczer, and Alessandro Flammini, "Online Human-Bot Interactions: Detection, Estimation, and Characterization," March 27, 2017, https://arxiv.org/pdf/1703.03107.pdf. (Note that Twitters' own estimate is 8.9 percent.) Facebook's statistics are taken from the Facebook website, https://transparency.facebook.com/community-standards-enforcement#fake-accounts.

5. Francis, "Message of His Holiness Pope Francis for World Communications Day," Libreria Editrice Vaticana, January 24, 2018, http://www.vatican.va/content/francesco/en/messages/communications/documents/papa-francesco_20180124_mes-saggio-comunicazioni-sociali.html.

6. Francis, "Message of His Holiness Pope Francis for World-Communications Day."

7. Jack Shafer, "Who Said It First? Journalism Is the 'First Rough Draft of History,'" *Slate*, August 30, 2010, https://slate.

com/news-and-politics/2010/08/on-the-trail-of-the-question-who-first-said-or-wrote-that-journalism-is-the-first-rough-draft-of-history.html.

8. Hiawatha Bray, "Survey Says: Many Americans Love Their Fake News," *Boston Globe,* January 17, 2020, https://www.bostonglobe.com/business/2020/01/17/survey-says-love-our-fake-news/kw0E8MYRpkH3LCJqJNe0nL/story.html.

3. Understand Bias

1. The term *echo chamber* applied to political discourse seems to have first been used by Kathleen Hall Jamieson and Joseph N. Capella in their 2008 book by that title, but it first came into vogue as relates to social media with Eli Pariser's TED talk, "Beware Online 'Filter Bubbles,'" in May 2011. See https://www.ted.com/talks/eli_pariser_beware_online_filter_bubbles?language=en.

2. Pariser, "Beware Online 'Filter Bubbles.'"

3. Kartik Hosanagar, "Blame the Echo Chamber on Facebook. But Blame Yourself, Too," *Wired*, November 25, 2016, https://www.wired.com/2016/11/facebook-echo-chamber/.

4. David Robson, "The Myth of the Online Echo Chamber," BBC, April 16, 2018, https://www.bbc.com/future/article/20180416-the-myth-of-the-online-echo-chamber.

5. John T. Jost and David M. Amodio, "Political Ideology as Motivated Social Cognition: Behavioral and Neuroscientific Evidence," *Motivation and Emotion* 36, no. 1 (2012): 55–64.

4. Value the Person

1. Fyodor Dostoevsky, *The Brothers Karamazov*, trans. Constance Garrett (New York: Lowell Press, 2009), 48.

2. See Matthew Green, "No Comment! Why More News Sites Are Dumping Their Comment Sections," *KQED News*, January 24, 2018, https://www.kqed.org/lowdown/29720/no-comment-why-a-growing-number-of-news-sites-are-dumping-their-comment-sections. See also the Reuters editor's note, "Reader Comments in the Age of Social Media," Reuters News Service, November 7, 2014, http://blogs.reuters.com/great-debate/2014/11/07/editors-note-reader-comments-in-the-age-of-social-media/.

3. For a helpful exploration of Christian thought on this topic, see George Weigel, "The Catholic Journey to Religious Freedom," *National Review*, December 20, 2017, https://www.nationalreview.com/2017/12/george-weigel-religious-freedom-institute-speech/.

4. Roger Fisher and William Ury, *Getting to Yes: Negotiating Agreement without Giving In* (New York: Penguin, 1991), 3–14.

5. See the *Hidden Brain* podcast, "When It Comes to Politics and 'Fake News' Facts Aren't Enough," March 13, 2017, https://www.npr.org/2017/03/13/519661419/when-it-comes-to-politics-and-fake-news-facts-arent-enough. For a lovely example of someone who had their worldview shifted through generous conversation, see the *On Being* podcast, "Derek Black and Matthew Stevenson: Befriending Radical Disagreement," May 17, 2018, https://onbeing.org/programs/derek-black-and-matthew-stevenson-befriending-radical-disagreement/.

5. Lead with Curiosity

1. Augustine of Hippo, *De Diversis*, 83.71.5.

2. J. Nathan Matias, "Posting Rules in Science Discussions Prevents Problems & Increases Participation," *Civil Servant*, April 29, 2019, https://civilservant.io/moderation_experiment_r_science_rule_posting.html.

3. Sarah Perez, "Twitter's Doubling of Character Count from 140 to 280 Had Little Impact on Length of Tweets," *TechCrunch,* October 30, 2018, https://techcrunch.com/2018/10/30/twitters-doubling-of-character-count-from-140-to-280-had-little-impact-on-length-of-tweets/.

4. Erin E. Buckels, Paul D. Trapnell, and Delroy L. Paulhus, "Trolls Just Want to Have Fun," *Journal of Personality and Individual Differences* 67 (September 2014): 97–102. For a helpful overview, see "Internet Trolls: Born That Way?," found at https://youtu.be/YLggqoPEfJU.

5. Justin Cheng, Cristian Danescu-Niculescu-Mizil, Jure Leskovec, and Michael Bernstein, "Anyone Can Become a Troll: Causes of Trolling Behavior in Online Discussions," *Proceedings of the 2017 ACM Conference on Computer Supported Cooperative Work and Social Computing* (New York: ACM, 2017), 1217–30.

6. For a summary of this research, see the Center for Countering Digital Hate, "Don't Feed the Trolls: How to Deal with Hate on Social Media," 2019, https://www.counterhate.co.uk/dont-feed-the-trolls.

7. I was introduced to this Shaw quote by the Center for Countering Digital Hate, https://www.counterhate.co.uk/.

8. https://www.counterhate.co.uk/.

6. Talk about Intent and Impact

1. There are a number of sources that make a similar point, but I was first introduced to the concept by Douglas Stone, Bruce Patton, and Sheila Heen, *Difficult Conversations: How to Discuss What Matters Most* (New York: Penguin, 2010), 44–57.

2. Stone, Patton, and Heen, *Difficult Conversations: How to Discuss What Matters Most*, 39–40.

3. *Hidden Brain* podcast, "Screaming Into the Void: How Outrage Is Hijacking Our Culture, and Our Minds," October 7, 2019, https://www.npr.org/transcripts/767186846. For greater depth, see William J. Brady, Ana P. Gattman, and Jay J. Van Bavel, "Attentional Capture Helps Explain Why Moral and Emotional Content Go Viral," accessed through the National Institutes of Health, https://www.ncbi.nlm.nih.gov/pubmed/31486666.

4. For a definition of the term *influencer*, see "What Is an Influencer?," Influencer Marketing Hub, https://influencermarketinghub.com/what-is-an-influencer/.

5. As an example, see Lindsay Dodgson, "27 Times Influencers Were Called Out for Controversies and Weird Behavior in 2019," *Insider*, December 28, 2019, https://www.insider.com/influencers-who-got-called-out-for-controversies-behavior-in-2019.

7. Privilege Face-to-Face Encounter

1. Lee Rainie and Kathryn Zickuhr, "Americans' Views on Mobile Etiquette," Pew Research Center, August 26, 2015,

https://www.pewresearch.org/internet/2015/08/26/americans-views-on-mobile-etiquette/.

2. Andrew Przybyliski and Netta Weinstein, "Can You Connect with Me Now? How the Presence of Mobile Communication Technology Influences Face-to-Face Conversation Quality," *Journal of Social and Personal Relationships* 30, no. 3 (2013), available at https://journals.sagepub.com/doi/full/10.1177/0265407512453827.

3. Sherry Turkle, preface to the 2017 edition of *Alone Together: Why We Expect More from Technology and Less from Each Other* (New York: Basic Books, 2017), accessed as an e-book.

4. This point of view, represented by any number of people, is argued well by Sr. Theresa Aletheia Noble, FSP. See "Friendship in a Digital Age Panel," DeNicola Center for Ethics and Culture, University of Notre Dame, November 26, 2019, https://www.youtube.com/watch?v=qFbolbNqoRk&list=PLY7_UvAXIWymN3EdNcYClNdL33N4eoH2W&index=6&t=0s.

5. I think of the letter here between Bl. Jordan of Saxony and his dear friend, Dominican prioress Diana d'Andalo: "O Diana, how miserable is the present state which we must endure since we cannot love one another without sorrow or think of one another without anxiety! Who shall lead us . . . into the City of the Lord of Hosts, where we shall sigh no more, sighing neither after the Most High, nor for one another?" See Paul Burns, *Butler's Saint for the Day* (Collegeville, MN: Liturgical Press, 2007), 73.

6. This metaphor is borrowed from Fr. Anthony Sciapparra. See "Friendship in a Digital Age Panel."

7. Francis, "Message of His Holiness Pope Francis for the 53rd World Communications Day," Libreria Editrice Vaticana, January 24, 2019, http://www.vatican.va/content/francesco/en/messages/communications/documents/papa-francesco_20190124_messaggio-comunicazioni-sociali.html.

8. Sherry Turkle, introduction to the 2017 edition of *Alone Together*.

9. Robin Dunbar in Maria Koonikova, "The Limits of Friendship," *New Yorker*, October 7, 2014, http://www.newyorker.com/science/maria-konnikova/social-media-affect-math-dunbar-number-friendships.

10. Dunbar in Koonikova, "Limits of Friendship." See also the study by Charles Croom, Bay Gross, Larry D. Rosen, and Brad Rosen, "What's Her Face(book)? How Many of Their Facebook 'Friends' Can College Students Actually Identify?," *Computers in Human Behavior,* November 2016, https://dl.acm.org/doi/10.1016/j.chb.2015.11.015. Key finding: The survey group could only match names with faces for 72.2 percent of their Facebook friends, even after allowed to participate in the exercises multiple times.

11. Dunbar in Koonikova, "Limits of Friendship."

8. Manage Your Energy

1. Data culled from the marketing research websites Global Web Index and Statista, then reported in Marie Ennis-O'Connor, "How Much Time Do People Spend on Social Media in 2019?," *Medium*, August 8, 2019, https://medium.com/@JBBC/how-much-time-do-people-spend-on-social-me-

dia-in-2019-infographic-cc02c63bede8. See also, "Average Time Spent Daily on Social Media (Latest 2020 Data)," *Broadband Search*, https://www.broadbandsearch.net/blog/average-daily-time-on-social-media#post-navigation-7.

2. Ennis-O'Connor, "How Much Time Do People Spend on Social Media in 2019?" See also Colin Hebblethwaite, "The Average Person Has 7 Social Media Accounts," *Tech Marketing*, November 17, 2017, https://marketingtechnews.net/news/2017/nov/17/average-person-has-7-social-media-accounts/.

3. US Bureau of Labor Statistics, "Economic News Release, Table 12. Average Hours per Day Spent in Primary Activities for the Civilian Population, 2018 Quarterly and Annual Averages," last modified June 19, 2019, https://www.bls.gov/news.release/atus.t12.htm; "Average Time Spent Daily on Social Media," *Broadband Search*.

4. "In real life, it's estimated that people talk about themselves around 30 to 40% of the time; however, social media is all about showing off one's life and accomplishments, so people talk about themselves a staggering 80% of the time." See "What Is Social Media Addiction?," Addiction Center, https://www.addictioncenter.com/drugs/social-media-addiction/.

5. There are multiple articles on this phenomenon. For a summary of the research, see Trevor Haynes with Rebecca Clements, "Dopamine, Smartphones & You: A Battle for Your Time," *Science in the News* (blog), Harvard University, May 1, 2018, http://sitn.hms.harvard.edu/flash/2018/dopamine-smartphones-battle-time/.

6. A key voice in this area of research has been Professor Larry Rosen of California State University. See Angie Marcos,

"Are You Addicted to Your Smart Phone?," *California State University News*, April 26, 2017, https://www2.calstate.edu/csu-system/news/Pages/are-you-addicted-to-your-smartphone.aspx, and Larry Rosen, "Relax, Turn Off Your Phone, and Go to Sleep," *Harvard Business Review*, August 31, 2015, https://hbr.org/2015/08/research-shows-how-anxiety-and-technology-are-affecting-our-sleep.

7. J. Clement, "Share of Online Users in the United States Who Report Being Addicted to Social Media as of April 2019, by Age Group," *Statista*, December 10, 2019, https://www.statista.com/statistics/1081292/social-media-addiction-by-age-usa/.

8. Abraham Joshua Heschel, prologue and part one of *The Sabbath* (New York: Farrar, Straus, and Giroux, 1951).

9. J. Clement, "Device Usage of Facebook Users Worldwide as of April 2020," *Statista*, April 24, 2020, https://www.statista.com/statistics/377808/distribution-of-facebook-users-by-device/.

10. Stefan Natter, "I Turned My iPhone Screen Gray for One Month—Here Is Why," *Medium*, January 15, 2017, https://medium.com/@natterstefan/i-turned-my-iphone-screen-gray-for-one-month-here-is-why-c9b6c8221051; *CBS This Morning* interview with Tristan Harris, "Silicon Valley Insider on Why Smartphones Are 'Slot Machines,'" April 10, 2017, https://www.youtube.com/watch?time_continue=2&v=gvQxtotEX-M&feature=emb_logo.

11. Emily McFarlan Miller, "The Science of 'Technology Shabbat': Observing the Sabbath to Rediscover Rest—and Claim Its Benefits," *National Catholic Reporter Online*, July 8, 2019, https://www.ncronline.org/news/media/science-technology-shabbat.

12. For an enjoyable article on various ways of limiting one's social media usage, see Sarah K. Peck, "I Ran 4 Experiments to Break My Social Media Addiction. Here's What Worked," *Harvard Business Review,* October 18, 2018, https://hbr.org/2018/10/i-ran-4-experiments-to-break-my-social-media-addiction-heres-what-worked.

Epilogue

1. Francis, "Message of His Holiness Pope Francis for World Communications Day," Libreria Editrice Vaticana, January 24, 2018, http://www.vatican.va/content/francesco/en/messages/communications/documents/papa-francesco_20180124_messaggio-comunicazioni-sociali.html.

Ann M. Garrido is associate professor of homiletics at Aquinas Institute of Theology in St. Louis, Missouri, where she previously directed the school's Doctorate of Ministry in Preaching program. Garrido has served as the Marten Faculty Fellow in Homiletics at the University of Notre Dame. She is the author of seven books, including the award-winning *Redeeming Administration*, *Redeeming Conflict*, and *Let's Talk About Truth*. She travels nationally and internationally helping communities discuss the topics they find toughest to talk about—conversations that always involve questions of truth.

anngarrido.com
Facebook: anngarridodmin